Case method
in management development

Case method
in management development
Guide for effective use

John I. Reynolds

Management Development Series No. 17
International Labour Office   Geneva

ISBN 92-2-102363-X

First published 1980
Fourth impression 1989

Printed in the German Democratic Republic

CONTENTS

PART IV - CASE METHOD TEACHING SYSTEM COMPONENTS

The case method is based on the belief that participants in management education and training programmes - both undergraduate students and practising executives with managerial experience - can efficiently improve their understanding of the management process and enhance their competence by studying, contemplating and discussing actual situations. The rigorous analysis required, especially in the longer and complex cases, is said to develop the skills of logical thinking, of searching for relevant information, of analysing and evaluating facts and of drawing conclusions needed for managerial decisions. The experience it gives in arguing a viewpoint before one's peers also develops the ability to communicate clearly, to consider the views of others and to arrive at solutions that would gain collective support.

For a number of years the best management development professionals have, therefore, made extensive use of case studies in their teaching and training programmes. Indeed, following the pioneering example of the Harvard University Graduate School of Business Administration, a number of management educators have demonstrated their faith in the case method by successfully teaching management and administration courses by this method alone.

Within the last 15-20 years management educators have made a considerable effort to enrich the store of teaching and training methods, in particular to deal with certain aspects and situations for which, as they have found, the case method is not fully comprehensive. For example, if a case is taught it is the author of the case and not the student who has actually collected the facts in the organisation concerned by the case. And, after having studied and discussed a case, the trainee does not have to implement his decision and live with its consequences; some participants, it is argued, would actually

1

behave quite differently in discussing a case if they knew that they would also be responsible for implementing the conclusions.

Management education and training in the 1980s will, therefore, be using a mix of methods and techniques, with a growing emphasis on live problem analysis and problem solving, practically useful projects, teamwork and team building, organisation development, accelerated transfer of relevant experience and, in particular, the individual manager's responsibility for his own self-development.

The case method will have a very important role to play in this process; thousands of new cases will be needed and thousands of management teachers and trainers will have to master the skills of case teaching and case writing, as well as of aptly combining the case method with other methods and techniques. Nowhere in the world is the case method likely to make a greater contribution to management education than in developing countries and regions; yet it is in those very regions where the fewest cases have as yet been written and where too many management teachers and trainers feel uneasy about using or writing a case.

This manual has been written within the framework of the ILO Management Development Programme with a view to helping management institutions, individual teachers and trainers as well as participants in management programmes to use the case method more extensively and more effect-ively. The author, Professor John I. Reynolds, of the Texas A and M University, is himself an experienced case teacher and case writer; for many years he has used the method and trained case writers not only in the USA, but in several developing countries as well.

Audience

The case method is effective when it is understood and correctly used at several levels.

First of all, there are those who are supposed to learn by case method - the participants in teaching and training programmes. They may be students in univer-sities and graduate schools of business and public admin-istration, junior managers interested in longer manage-ment development programmes, or rather experienced managers attending senior and top management seminars and similar programmes of relatively short duration. They are all interested in studying relevant cases in a way that helps to increase their knowledge and skills, al-though an experienced manager will, as a rule, need to study a case which is different from that presented to persons without any business and administrative experience. In Part I the book addresses itself to course participants. They are called students in most cases; the term student is used here as a generic term and could be supplemented or replaced by terms such as trainees or participants.

The second level includes the teachers. The success of case study teaching depends on their case teaching and case writing competence. Here again, the term teacher stands also for trainers, instructors, course and seminar leaders and other persons responsible for introducing and using cases in teaching and training programmes. Part II (Teaching by case method) and Part III (Case writing) have been written primarily for them. The assumption has been that they already know the subject-matter and how to solve problems and make decisions, but that they should learn more about how to use cases and how to write new cases.

Finally, it would hardly be possible to make good progress in teaching by case method and producing relevant local case material without adequate support of institutions and organisations where the method is used; and by this we mean, above all, the support provided by persons who manage educational and training institutions in the field of management and administration. This concerns heads (directors, managers, deans, principals, etc.) of institutions, directors of training and research, members of scientific or pedagogic councils and other policy-making bodies in institutions and so on. Training directors in business and other organisations might find this part useful as well.

Uses of the book

The first possible use is reading for self-development. Anybody who falls in the categories mentioned above may find this useful if he is looking for practical guidance and references related to the case method.

The second possible use is in connection with workshops and seminars aimed at enhancing learning and teaching skills. To facilitate this the manual has been structured in four parts, each focused on a particular aspect or level of using and supporting the method. In summary form this approach is represented in figure 1. However, the reader should keep in mind that in designing training-of-trainers or similar programmes using this manual he has several options.

Figure 1 Suggestions for using this manual

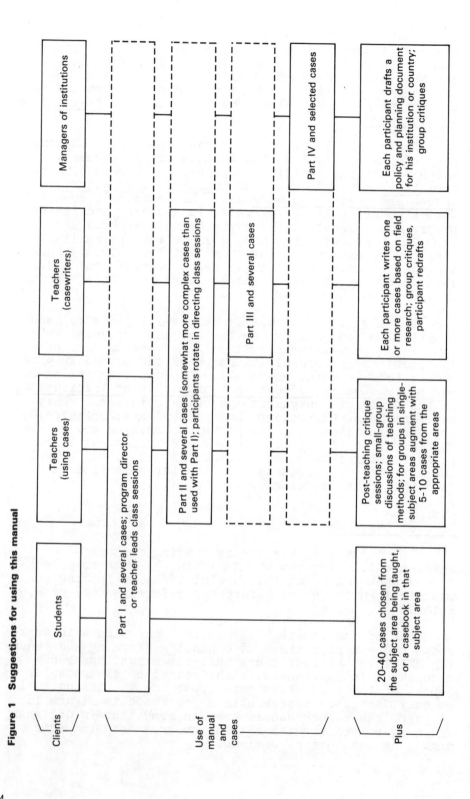

Clients	Students	Teachers (using cases)	Teachers (casewriters)	Managers of institutions
Use of manual and cases	Part I and several cases; program director or teacher leads class sessions			
		Part II and several cases (somewhat more complex cases than used with Part I); participants rotate in directing class sessions		
			Part III and several cases	Part IV and selected cases
Plus	20–40 cases chosen from the subject area being taught, or a casebook in that subject area	Post-teaching critique sessions; small-group discussions of teaching methods; for groups in single-subject areas augment with 5–10 cases from the appropriate areas	Each participant writes one or more cases based on field research; group critiques, participant redrafts	Each participant drafts a policy and planning document for his institution or country; group critiques

4

Students would normally concentrate on Part I in order to get advice on how to study a case, on a general-purpose problem-solving format, on participation in class discussions and on writing report papers. Chapters 1 through 4 would normally be assigned for reading by students, although Chapter 4 might be withheld until just before the first assignment of written work in the course.

Teachers of management and administration will be interested mainly in Part II and Part III, although in programmes where teachers are participants one would normally assign Part I at the beginning, and introduce at least certain elements of Part IV should this help to promote the method in various countries or institutions. The key decision will concern the use of Part II and Part III: teachers' training will concentrate on Part II, while workshops for case study writers will have to include both Part II and Part III.

Managers of management institutions and other individuals responsible for policy questions in teaching and training will seldom participate in a workshop dealing with the case method exclusively. The relevant parts of the book can be brought to their attention in various ways: for example, they can be invited to certain sessions in a training-of-trainers programme; or questions of promoting and supporting effective training methodology can be handled in various meetings and workshops gathering heads of institutions from various countries.

Several cases and some information materials are reproduced in the appendix part of the manual. This has been done in order to help both the individual reader, and the teachers' trainer looking for case material that could be used in teachers' or case writers' workshops. Notwithstanding this, readers should feel free to make their own selection and use cases that, according to their own judgement, are best suited for such purposes.

. Although at various places in this manual the author mentions that both the practices and philosophies of case method adherents differ concerning many points covered here, it is perhaps well to emphasise at the outset that no attempt has been made to cover every viewpoint. The author's preferences have dictated what is said. Good case method teachers and administrators will proceed to use and write cases as they please. The case method will not only survive such differences of opinion, but will thus become richer and better adapted to the many settings in which it is to be used.

PART I

STUDENTS' INTRODUCTION TO CASE METHOD

INTRODUCTION TO PART I

The definition of case method starts with the definition of a case. A case is a short description, in words and numbers, of an actual management situation. Most cases stop short of presenting all of the actions taken by the manager in the real-world situation. They thus leave open to the student the selection of actions which should be taken. It is expected that students will study cases, come to their own conclusions about what should be done, and then discuss the cases in class and/or write papers describing and defending their suggested courses of action. A case that deals with facts facing a financial officer of a firm allows the student to develop skill in making financial decisions. Cases that present marketing facts or production facts lead to decisions of the sort made by marketing or productions managers, and so on. A good case almost puts the student into the position of the real-world manager, facing the challenge to make a decision and prepare a plan of action.

"Case method" involves several additional concepts and activities which may not be very obvious to you as the student. The first of these is the teacher's selection of a sequence of cases to make up a course of study. It goes without saying that cases should be selected from the topic area of interest, such as "marketing", "accounting" or "production". This assists students in identifying typical problems in specific functional areas of management. A more difficult problem in sequencing is to select cases that build on one another. Partly, this is a matter of starting with easy cases and progressing to harder ones. But it also involves the order of introduction of ideas and analytical concepts.

A second major step in converting individual cases into "case method" is providing for feedback to the

student.   It is not enough to say that you, the student
will learn how to make decisions purely by studying cases
and thinking deeply about them.   You must get feedback
about the quality of your analysis and the probable value
of your plan of action.   Case method provides for this
in two ways, through feedback from student to student and
from teacher to student.   During the open discussion in
class each student can compare his/her analysis with those
of other students.   Particularly when students have had
some real-world experience, the varieties of experience
among the students themselves provide for very effective
feedback.   The teacher, as well, bears a special responsibility to assure you that your ideas are appraised.
Both in oral classroom discussions and written papers,
the teacher must provide feedback and comment on how your
ideas could be improved.

A final step in converting a series of cases into
case method teaching and learning is to draw out and
clarify the general concepts involved in clusters of
cases.   Usually the students will do most of this themselves, but alert teachers will make sure that it is done
as a matter of course.

If you as a student are asked to learn the skills of
management through case method, you deserve to know why
it is a valuable technique as well as how to do it.   You
will come to realise that case method demands more intense
involvement on your part, as compared with other common
forms of learning.   Not only will you be asked to learn
and understand ideas.   You will be asked to use the ideas
in appraising case situations; you will be making decisions and defending them in class.   It is a fair question
to ask, "Why should I go to the extra work of learning by
the case method?"

One way of learning skills is to come to understand
a number of common concepts about management and decision-
making.   A "concept" is any special way of fitting together facts and ideas which is useful in making sense
out of the complexities that surround us.   In the field
of management, for example, there is a concept called
"break-even analysis".   This concept shows the manager
how to arrange the facts about expected costs and selling
prices in such a way as to predict how many items must be
produced and sold before the enterprise will begin to
show a profit.   Many other concepts, some simpler and
others much more complex than break-even analysis, have
been developed in the field of management.   Why not just
list out the concepts in textbooks and lectures, with
examples to demonstrate their applications?   This is a
challenge to case method teaching which has been made not
only by students but by educators who prefer other teaching methods.

10

Answers to this challenge are largely pragmatic.
"Case method works" is the underlying theme of most
answers.   Its advocates cite the success of managers who
are graduates of case method programmes.   There are five
primary reasons why the method works:

- Student's find case method generally more interesting
  than pure lectures and textbook courses.   Therefore
  they willingly spend more time in studying.   This
  extra studying and thinking about management results
  in more learning.

- Students are more likely to remember ideas and concepts that they themselves evolved and used during
  the "experience" of solving real-world problems.

- Students develop skills in appraising situations and
  applying concepts rather than merely learning the
  concepts from textbook examples which are often very
  different from real-world situations.   It is said
  that case method better develops such skills.

- Students find that the group work and inter-action
  with other students called for by case method are an
  effective preparation for the human side of management.

- Students of case method learn how to develop new
  concepts, as well as to apply established concepts.
  Because tomorrow's problems are likely to call for
  new concepts, case method students tend to be better
  prepared for the future than those who merely have
  memorised existing concepts.

Apart from the concepts and skills you will learn
from the ongoing case method course which you are about
to start, there are several instructions you will find
useful:

- how to study a case,

- a general-purpose problem-solving format,

- how to participate in a case class discussion, and

- how to write a case analysis paper.

Each of these topics is a subject of one of the next four
chapters.

HOW TO STUDY A CASE

1

It should go without saying that case method requires students to do most of their studying before class, as contrasted with lecture method, in which most of the study occurs later, as class notes are reviewed. If you are going to understand fully the arguments and presentations of your fellow students in class, not to mention give a good presentation of your own, you must be prepared beforehand. In effect, you must place yourself in the role of the responsible manager in the case, and make the decision and plan the action called for by the facts as you interpret them.

The typical case consists of a number of pages of prose description. It often includes some quantitative material, either interspersed with the qualitative prose or presented as charts, graphs or tables. Other exhibits such as maps, organisation charts or factory layout plans may also be included. In fact, cases may include almost any type of material that can be printed, such as might be found in the manager's daily work. Some elaborate cases have been augmented by actual samples of the products involved, motion pictures showing the real scene and audio tapes of conversations. In some training programmes the entire class may visit a business site, thus involving all the students in the "case discovery" experience. The richer the case material, of course, the more involved can be the analysis by the student. What follows, however, deals with how to study a typical case, where all the information is in printed form.

There are several conventions of case writing which it is important for you as a student to understand. The need for such conventions arises because the case writer has, in a sense, represented you at the scene of the case. Since you were not present in person to judge the facts, the case writer must signal to you the quality of the evidence or facts on which your appraisal must be based.

Any simple declaration such as "the XYZ Company was founded in 1932", or "the firm had been continually profitable between 1941 and 1972" you may accept as "true", in the sense that, had you been gathering the information for yourself, this is what you would have discovered. A statement like, "the salesroom appeared nearly empty at the time of the case writer's visit" is another kind of "true" statement, yet it allows you to question, by analysing other case evidence, whether the period of the case writer's visit was typical of affairs in general.

Another substantial class of evidence is that which represents the opinions of people involved in the case situation (what may be called the "case characters"). The case writer wants you to know about these opinions, since such ideas often are very powerful in explaining what happens later on. But you must be careful not to accept such opinions as "true facts" until and unless your study of other evidence in the case leads you to accept the opinions as if they were facts. The case writer signals such opinions to you in several ways. The first is by direct quotations, enclosed in quotation marks. Particularly in cases that deal in detail with human relations a good many of the words in the case may be quotations, perhaps as the record of a conversation, the record of statements made in a committee meeting, and so on. A second form of attribution of opinion is such a statement as "Mr. Boss believed that his firm's principal strength was its aggressive sales force".

A third kind of evidence often found in cases is financial information, such as balance sheets and operating statements. Although you should not be unduly suspicious of these facts, particularly if it is clear that they are drawn from audited annual reports, it is well to remember that these, too, are a kind of "fact" that the case writer has had to accept on someone else's word. It is generally well understood in the USA, for example, that the "bottom line", or the net profit after tax, is heavily influenced by the assumptions underlying the operating statement, particularly assumptions about the rate of depreciation and about the value of inventory. As you study these facts you will have the responsibility to judge for yourself what they mean.

Another common convention is for cases to be written in the past tense. This is done so that an appropriate date can be used for the case event (e.g., "In October 1976 Mr. Kohan was studying his firm's sales figures") without making the tense seem artificial when the case is used at a later date. This "dating" of cases is important in some instances where generally well-recognised external events (such as wars, periods of economic recession or energy crises) are relevant to the case.

Steps in case study

Read the case through once, very quickly. The purpose of this reading is to make you familiar with the topic, the "cast of characters", the leading actor whose role you will play as you analyse the case, the general nature and quality of the evidence with which you must work, and some idea of the problem or problems that must be solved. This quick reading is like the first approach to a new city, in which you quickly identify major roads, shopping areas and office buildings, but leave until the second visit the details of your own involvement with the city.

Read the case thoroughly a second time, at a much slower and more thoughtful rate. Take note of important facts in the prose passages, and study each quantitative exhibit to decide what important fact or facts can be identified there. By the end of the second reading of the case, you should be able to abstract from the case a statement of the problem(s) involved, the nature of the decision(s) facing the manager, and most of the major elements (constraints, opportunities and resources) which influence the actions the manager can take.

Finally, recheck the various important facts you have previously identified, to make sure that your view of the situation is consistent with all the facts. It is at this point that you will prepare your analysis and recommendations using either the general-purpose problem-solving format described in the next chapter or some more specific analytical technique that you have learned in previous courses or in earlier sessions of the present course.

A GENERAL-PURPOSE PROBLEM-SOLVING FORMAT 2

All modern concepts of managerial problem solving have several common elements:

- identifying the problem(s) or areas for improvement;

- setting objectives or goals for achievement (introducing a standard of values or criterion by which improvement is to be measured);

- identifying possible alternative courses of action;

- predicting the likely outcomes or consequences of each course of action (using the ideas of "cause and effect" and "probability"); and

- choosing and implementing the course of action whose expected outcome most nearly matches or exceeds the desired outcome or objective.

Some specific concepts, such as linear programming to allocate scarce resources, achieve mathematical precision by ignoring many qualitative facts in the situation being analysed. Such simplification allows those mathematical models and formulae to be solved for "the best solution to this (simplified) problem". In contrast, many real-world situations are too complex to assert that there is only one "correct" solution. The best one may say, perhaps, is that a suggested course of action can be supported by effective logical argument. The "format" shown in figure 2 and its description fits any case situation. It does not, of course, guarantee that the student will think of all possible alternatives or even that all students will identify the same problems or adopt the same objectives.

Figure 2 A general-purpose problem-solving format

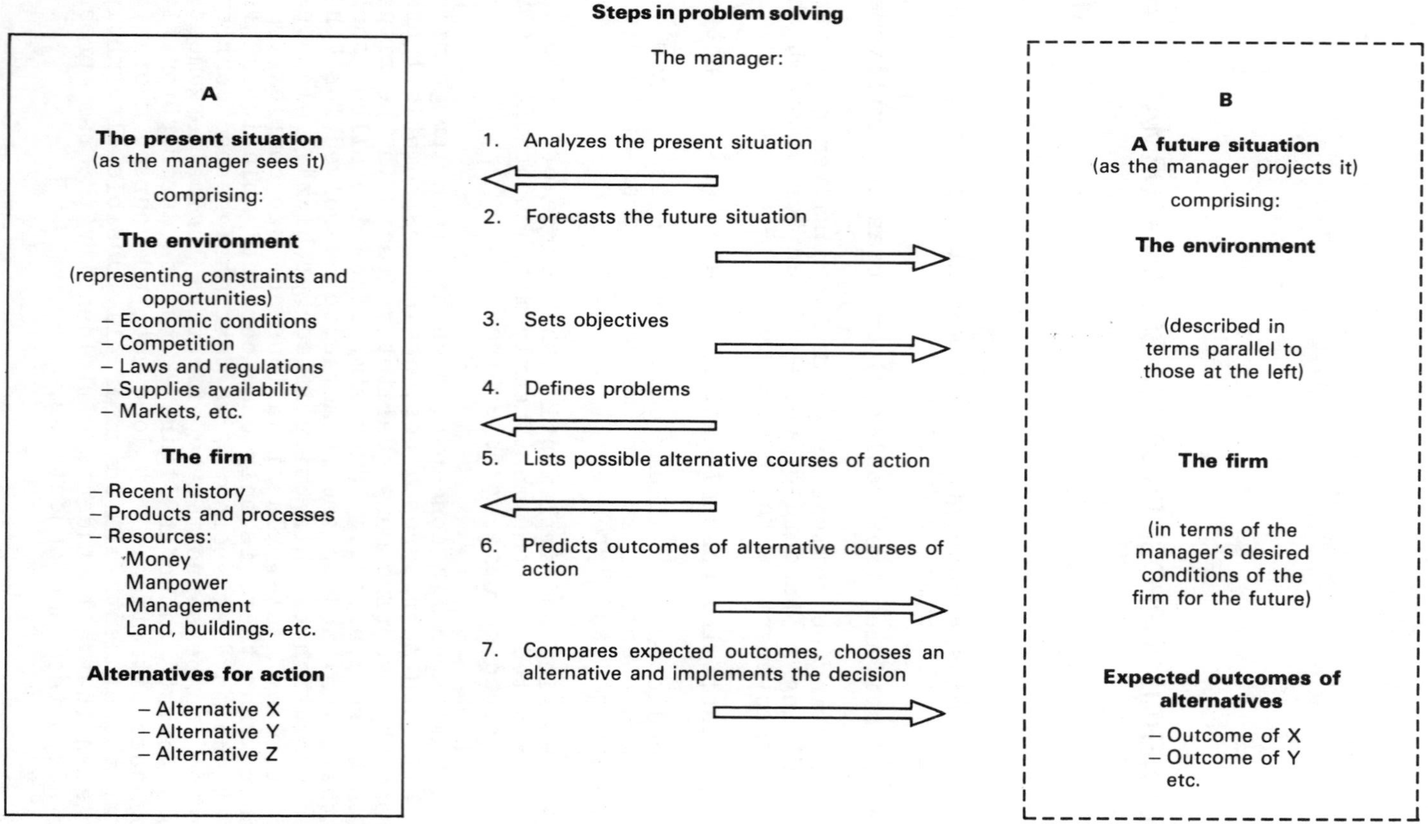

Steps in problem solving

The manager:

1. Analyzes the present situation

2. Forecasts the future situation

3. Sets objectives

4. Defines problems

5. Lists possible alternative courses of action

6. Predicts outcomes of alternative courses of action

7. Compares expected outcomes, chooses an alternative and implements the decision

---

A

The present situation
(as the manager sees it)

comprising:

The environment
(representing constraints and opportunities)
– Economic conditions
– Competition
– Laws and regulations
– Supplies availability
– Markets, etc.

The firm
– Recent history
– Products and processes
– Resources:
  ·Money
  Manpower
  Management
  Land, buildings, etc.

Alternatives for action
– Alternative X
– Alternative Y
– Alternative Z

B

A future situation
(as the manager projects it)

comprising:

The environment

(described in terms parallel to those at the left)

The firm

(in terms of the manager's desired conditions of the firm for the future)

Expected outcomes of alternatives
– Outcome of X
– Outcome of Y
  etc.

Description of the problem-solving format

The following letters and numerals refer to those shown on figure 2. The description should be read in conjunction with the diagram.

A. **The present situation** (as the manager sees it). This box in the diagram represents all facts about the problem situation, including past and present. In the real world there could be an immense amount of detail. Managers cannot pay attention to everything. They therefore do some simplifying; they solve problems as they see them. For you, as a case method student, the contents of box A are presented in the form of the case. The case writer has selected the facts to put into the case. You are expected to treat the facts of the written case in the same way the manager treats the facts of the present situation.

B. **A future situation** (as the manager projects it). This box in the diagram is surrounded by a dashed line to emphasise that it is a product of the manager's thoughts. Every manager must learn to think effectively about the unknown future. This problem-solving method requires one to create a special image of the future, in order to compare it with the present situation. You, as a student, will find it useful to practice the technique of designing a projection of the future, based on case situations, as you follow the steps in problem solving. For convenience, all of the instructions below are expressed in terms of solving <u>case</u> problems; you are the manager.

Steps in problem solving

Step 1. **Analyse the present situation.** The careful study of the case described in Chapter 1 constitutes this analysis. What you are seeking as you analyse the case is an understanding about how facts are related in the particular case situation. What are the primary causes of cost for the firm? How intense is the competition? Are the firm's customers more interested in the quality or in the price of the product?

All of these questions, and the many others you might ask yourself as you study the case, are questions about <u>cause</u> and <u>effect</u>. As you put facts together in new and different ways, you are deciding what <u>causes</u> are having <u>effects</u> on the firm. Your attention may be directed to a particular relationship by some theory you have been taught. When this happens, you are gaining experience in applying known concepts to new situations.

When you examine relationships about which you have not previously been taught, you are gaining experience in developing new concepts.

A facet of every case situation is the environment, which represents constraints and opportunities for the firm. Sometimes many environmental facts will be specified in the case itself. As was noted earlier, however, sometimes the environment is implied by the mere fact that a case is located in a particular region at a particular date. For example, a marketing case set in the United States in 1979 has an environment full of television advertising, nearly universal literacy and many print media for advertising, a high average standard of living and highly active competition for every consumer product. By contrast, a case about the manufacturer of a consumer product in a developing country would have an entirely different environment. The constraints on action and opportunities would be quite different. This is one reason why case writing efforts are currently going on in all regions of the world. Different environments make different problems arise even when other facts of the situation are similar.

Step 2. <u>Forecast the future situation</u>. The future situation contains a great many circumstances over which the individual manager cannot hope to exert much control. Most environmental facts, for example, are beyond the manager's direct control. In this step, you, as the manager, forecast what will happen in order to help you identify the future constraints and opportunities affecting the outcomes of your planned actions. What facts it is important to forecast differ from case to case. Any environmental fact you have found to be important in the present situation should appear in your forecast.

This forecasting step is less important and easier when the case deals with short-range (i.e., less than one year) problem solving. In many such instances it is safe to assume no change in the relevant environment over a short time interval from analysis to decision to action.

Step 3. <u>Set objectives</u>. At this stage of the problem-solving process, it is possible to demonstrate specifically what is meant by setting objectives. An objective is a desired future state of the firm, described in terms of those effects which the manager can influence. It is often said that objectives should be stated in such terms that you can <u>measure</u> results to see if the objectives have been accomplished. They should also be given in terms of a date for completion. Both these requirements can be fulfilled in the format shown here.

Setting objectives for short-range problems may be reasonably simple. For example, if the "problem" in a factory is that the production rate has fallen from the standard rate of 4,000 units per day to 3,000 units, your objective may be "to return to the standard rate of production within five days". As another example, a short-range objective may be "to reduce the scrap rate from the present 8% to 5%, by the end of the next accounting period".

In more complex problems and those involving long-range planning, objectives often contain more elements. They may involve changes in scale of operations, changes in selling prices, new product lines, increased manpower and other variables under the control of the manager. The details to be itemised in the "desired future conditions of the enterprise" are any which are relevant for the argument being made in each instance.

Step 4. Define problems. It may seem strange to delay defining the problems to this late stage in the format. This delay is important, however, the problems can now be defined in ways which assure you that you will think of effective actions to solve them. Problem statements now can be expressed in terms of the differences between the present situation and the desired future situation of the firm (the objectives). Following this line of thought often prevents a too-hasty acceptance of some surface fact of the present situation as being "the problem". Sometimes this too-hasty action has been called "treating the symptoms of the problem rather than the problem itself". In any event, by this stage in the process, one is ready to make a problem statement in terms that allow for later measurement of how well the problem has been solved.

Steps 5 and 6. List possible alternative courses of action and predict their outcomes. It is convenient to discuss the next two steps as if they were one, because you will discard a great many actions you might take immediately upon thinking about their probable consequences. Some cases contain a good deal of information about alternatives, just as is often true in the real world. For example, a salesman representing a machine tool manufacturer may appear at your door, offering to sell you a new machine that will increase your production rate without adding to your manpower requirements. Your problem is to decide between buying the new machine or continuing as you are. Your objectives might be stated as "to achieve a maximum return on invested capital". Therefore your prediction of "outcomes" would be in the form of comparable ratios of profits to money invested under the two alternatives: "buy the new machine" or "continue doing what we are doing now".

In other instances the case may be silent about potential alternatives and their outcomes. This is particularly true of cases dealing with human relationships. In these instances it will be up to you, the student, to devise alternatives and predict their outcomes. This is, after all, what the manager in the real world must do, when faced with such situations.

At the point of predicting outcomes there arises an important concern, the issue of uncertainty. We all know, by general experience, that we cannot be sure of any forecast of the future, or of the predicted outcome of any action. There is not room in this case method introduction to go into detail about ways to handle uncertainty. Suffice it to say that case method and the format here described are adaptable to any treatment of uncertainty that may be appropriate. Managers in the real world continually make decisions and take actions based upon their expected outcomes, whether their expectations have been developed intuitively or scientifically. What is important for you to keep in mind is that you must think explicitly about the outcome or consequences of each alternative course of action.

Step 7. <u>Compare, choose and implement</u>. This final step may almost appear to be trivial, once you have stated and ranked predicted outcomes in order of their attrativeness in terms of the objectives. This is especially true of instances where you have defined a single simple objective, such as "increase the output of the factory by 6%", or "improve the return on investment from 10% to 12%". If you are careful to make your predictions about outcomes in exactly these terms, the course of action which is "best" in meeting your objectives will be obvious.

In an instance of multiple objectives, however, the comparison and choice may require some special thought. For example, your objectives might be "to increase the output of the factory by 6% without increasing the labour force by more than four people". If you then are faced with a choice between two alternatives: (a) one which increases factory output by 7%, while requiring five extra workers, and (b) one which increases factory output by 5%, while requiring just four extra workers, you would need to decide which of your objectives was more important. In instances like this example, typically, you would try to combine the objectives in one overriding objective expressed in terms of "long-run profitability of the firm". In practice, it is sometimes impossible to express all your goals in terms of a single standard. Often, in countries which try to operate their industries on a "no-profit, no-loss" basis, the multiple goals, perhaps set by different ministries, force the manager to compromise.   It is this fact which makes the final step, "compare and choose", more than a trivial one.

In the case method the problem cannot be termed "solved" until some attention has been given to implementation.   It is fair to say that this is often the most difficult part of a plan to evaluate.   If it is hard to predict the outcome of <u>what one does</u>, it is even harder to predict the influence <u>of how one does it</u>.   For example, suppose that you had decided that the profitability of one factory in your company could only be assured by a reduction of 10% in its labour force. Whether you were able to choose to transfer the redundant staff to another factory, what criteria you applied for selecting the individuals to be transferred, in what way you decided to discuss the issue with the trade unions, etc., might make a great deal of difference to the outcome of your managerial action.

Once you have read and analysed a case in terms of the problem-solving framework suggested above, you are prepared either to participate in a class discussion of the case or to write a paper about the case.   Each of these activities is the subject of a following chapter.

HOW TO PARTICIPATE IN A CASE-CLASS DISCUSSION

3

Different teachers have different expectations about what should take place in class. Major differences surround the role of the individual student as contrasted to the role of groups of students. No one way is "right". Each style has its purpose and its parallel circumstances in the real world.

Purely individual responsibility

Each student prepares the case analysis without any pre-class discussion with other students. The class consists of presentations of one student viewpoint after another. Depending upon the teacher's preferences, students may be asked to make fairly detailed complete statements of their arguments, or they may be encouraged to offer shorter statements selected from their analyses, at appropriate points in the development of the class discussion. As an example of the latter, the first student to talk might be asked to "give the relevant facts about the current situation and a forecast of the future environment". Other students might be asked to add to or suggest different interpretations of the situation.

The technique of complete individual arguments from each student often results in a series of statements with many points in common, but each lacking breadth. Also, there will likely be quite substantial differences among interpretations of some case facts. On the other hand, building a case analysis bit by bit from selected inputs from each student adds breadth and emphasises the wide variety of ideas that can be identified in the case material. This second approach, however, may move too slowly to retain the interest of all students. Chances are that your teacher will use a combination of the two approaches. You should therefore feel comfortable if asked to present your full analysis and conclusions or if asked to probe deeply into the details of a part of your argument.

The eventual outcome of class discussions of individual efforts will usually be the development of consensus or general agreement about the relative merits of a small number of possible courses of action. Sometimes the class will develop a general preference for just one "solution", even though several different solutions may have been suggested by different individuals. Most frequently when this general agreement is reached it is because the discussion has helped the class to discover ingenious ways to incorporate the "best" parts of several individual suggestions into a single preferred solution.

This teaching technique is most closely parallel to a real-world committee meeting of department heads of equal status, discussing a common problem on which each committee member has been supplied with the same background information. The skills in analysis, decision making, oral presentation of your own position, and synthesis of a plan through compromise are all skills that are much in demand in the real world.

Individual inputs after
small group discussion

One very popular variant of the individual student responsibility model is for students to meet in small groups to discuss their individual analyses, prior to the class where the teacher is present. This small group meeting allows the individual to "try out" ideas before exposing them to the larger class group and the teacher. Persons who tend to be quiet in larger group meetings often feel comfortable in speaking out in small groups. In this method no attempt is made to force a consensus within the small groups. Each individual is independently responsible for later presenting ideas in the full class. Often small groups retain their identities throughout the course; the same three to six persons constitute a group for pre-class discussion of cases for weeks or months at a stretch. This continued contact is thought to encourage confidence on the part of shy participants and to take effective advantage of the differing strengths of various group members. For example, if a group contains a person with good accounting skills and another person with special sensitivity to personnel relations, each may learn much from the other in the pre-class discussions.

This variant has its parallel in the real world also. Often large group meetings will occur after a subject has been discussed avidly by small groups in an organisation. The annual meeting of a corporation could be handled this way. Periodic meetings of management people at various levels of the organisation, whose major purpose is to encourage all viewpoints to be expressed, also have this form. But perhaps the best example of such a process is the public forum in which citizens have the right to express their opinions on matters of mutual concern. They may well have met in small groups prior to the open meeting, yet each is speaking individually at the forum.

Group analysis, spokesperson presenters in class

Often the teacher may expect that the pre-class discussion groups will reach a consensus within each group and nominate a spokesperson (perhaps a different one each day from a group with continuing membership) to present that viewpoint in class. This cuts down on the number of individuals who speak out in each class, and should result in a longer time being available to hear each argument.

If the presentations are not scheduled in advance, the appearance of the class may be quite like those where individuals are responsible, except that fewer students will become involved. In extreme instances, the teacher may set up role-playing exercises, in which one group makes a formal presentation from the front of the classroom, and the other groups take the role of a critical audience, putting forward questions or counter-arguments.

This method of class operation is most closely parallel to real-world briefings of management by junior executives, or alternatively the presentations made by consultants to a firm's management.

The mechanics of participation

Whatever the style of participation, there remains the question of the mechanics of being recognised to participate in class. Once again, the preferences of the teacher will make a difference. Some teachers notify in advance the persons who are to recite. Others call on students at random, or use a pre-arranged "call list" without telling the students in what order they may be called upon. Most teachers at one time or another call upon students who raise their hands. Sometimes in the heat of discussion students will enter into the discussion spontaneously without waiting to be called upon. Your teacher should make it clear to you what process will be followed.

Finally, it should be recognised that each student is "participating" in the class even while remaining silent. You should be listening to every other student's contribution to the discussion, constantly comparing what is being said with your own ideas and analysis. In case method it is far less important for you to take notes for later review than it is to listen actively to what is being said, and plan your own next recitation. It is at this very point that the major difference between your learning knowledge, by being told something by a lecturer, and your learning skill, by practising the activities of decision making and persuasion, becomes apparent. You should remember that you are engaged in learning just as much while you are actively listening and following the line of others' argument, as you are when you are presenting your own ideas.

Sometimes the teacher will add to any of the above teaching plans for class discussion the requirement that a paper be written and handed in. How to prepare the written paper is the subject of the following chapter.

HOW TO WRITE A CASE-ANALYSIS PAPER

4

No matter what individual requirements regarding your paper's form and style may be set forth by your teacher, it is most important that your paper makes clear what you recommend and why you recommend it. The ability to get these two ideas across clearly and in few words has often been identified as one of the surest ways to succeed as a manager. What action you recommend can easily be identified as the choice arrived at in Step 5 of the problem-solving format presented in Chapter 2. This can usually be stated in very few words. Why you recommend the action is that your selected action is "best" in terms of the whole analytical plan you have carried out. How much of your reasoning needs to be repeated in the written paper depends on a number of factors:

- Whether your teacher has specified a maximum word limit for your paper.

- The extent to which your decision is based entirely on "case facts" as over against other research or your personal knowledge of the environment beyond what is given in the case. In general, references to "case facts" can be brief; most teachers are willing to assume that every reader of your paper will have read the case carefully. Thus your argument can focus on the inferences you have drawn from your combination of case facts. That is, upon your use of concepts. In contrast, where your argument is supported extensively by facts that are not in the case itself, you will need to introduce and qualify the facts.

- The extent to which your objectives and/or your value systems differ from the expected norm of the class. For example, if you are writing a paper about a US private enterprise firm, and you adopt the objective "maximising profitability", you need to write little justification for your general standards. Most American private enterprises are believed to operate according to such standards. However, if you believe that such a firm should, in the case at hand, "maximise social welfare", you should spend more time and words in justifying this less usual objective.

- The extent to which your predictions of the future and/or your expected outcomes of actions are "conventional" or "unconventional" in your own culture. It may be difficult to sense whether this is so in writing a paper (in making an oral presentation it is easier, since you have a chance to respond to questions). However, the more unconventional your thinking, the more you should expect to have to explain yourself.

Although your teacher should make clear the requirements regarding your paper's form, the following are generally useful guidelines for writing a case analysis report.

Prepare a summary statement, no more than one typewritten page in length, that clearly states what you recommend and the most important one or two reasons why. This summary statement will become the first sheet of your report. It is often said that busy real-world managers will refuse to read reports that are not accompanied by such summaries. It is also said that the busiest managers may not read anything but the summaries of reports. Whether or not these sayings are true of all cultures, the summary clearly is important. Although it will be presented as the first page of your report, you may in fact want to write it last, in order to be sure to make it as convincing as possible.

The body of your report may well follow some such outline as the problem-solving format suggested earlier, introducing ideas in the order shown below:

(i)   important facts about the present situation;

(ii)   forecast of changes in the situation;

(iii) objectives and goals for the future and the problem(s) which arise because the current situation falls short of future goals;

(iv)   alternative actions that might be taken, with predicted consequences of each alternative;

(v)   description in detail of the recommended action and its implementation.

Teachers differ in their preferences regarding what is "important" in section (i) above.   Some like a fairly detailed account of all the case facts that are later to be used in your argument.   Others prefer to shorten the first section, assuming that all readers of the report will have read the case.   For those who prefer only a short introduction, references to case facts would appear only at those places in the paper where they were especially pertinent to a point being made.   For example one might say, as part of an extended introduction, "The Kengolia Development Board (KDB) had attracted unfavourable comment in the public press because of its failure to pursue national objectives by developing new business enterprises."   If this were left out of a "shortened" introduction because it had been plainly stated in so many words in the case itself, it could later be incorporated as a part of the reasoning for a specific objective, put forward by the student.   Thus "the KDB should plan to establish five new enterprises in the coming year, to counteract the current impression that it is not active enough".

Throughout the paper, whether there is a word limit or not, you should make sure that you include only those ideas which help you explain what you recommend and why. If you find that certain case facts are irrelevant to your decision they should not be repeated in your paper. If you have based your decision on a single-valued objective, you need not specify all the other objectives you <u>might</u> have developed.   You should mention any truly supportable alternatives you considered and rejected, since you can often show in this way very effectively why you chose as you did.   But you should not try to include every conceivable alternative, including unrealistic ones, just out of a wish to appear "complete".   To describe an alternative in 50 words, only to demolish it in 10 words, is often called "setting up a straw man".   This means creating an artificial adversary, whose only importance is that he is easy to defeat.

Figures.   Many analyses involving mathematical comparisons and computation will be made much clearer by the use of tables, charts and diagrams.   If you use only one or two such devices in a paper, it is best to insert them in the text at the point where you refer to the ideas they demonstrate (as the author has done with figure 2 in Chapter 2).   If there are many such figures, it is better to put them in an appendix at the end of the paper, numbered in the order in which they are referred to.   Do not include figures to which you do not refer in the text of your paper.   In fact, unless you have at least a sentence or two of conclusions or inferences you have drawn from a figure (table, chart or diagram), probably the figure should be left out.

Appendices. If you need to add substantial material
to the case, such as newspaper articles describing environmental circumstances or long quoted references pertinent to the situation but not shown in the case, these
may be included as appendices to your report. Once
again, however, be sure that the point you are supporting
warrants all the extra reading you are requiring your
audience to do.

Summaries. Depending on the length of your report
you may need a short summary paragraph or two. Remember,
however, that your first page is itself a summary. If
your paper is no more than ten pages long, it will not
need a final summary.

The over-all criterion for a written report should
be your expected effect on your audience. Be as brief
as possible, given the level of understanding of your
audience, but make the paper long enough to persuade the
reader that your appraisal of the case is effective.

All of case method learning is best done by
experience; that is, in fact, the major message of these
first four chapters. Analyse a case and participate in
a class discussion. Receive feedback and try again.
Write a case analysis report. Receive feedback and try
again. We have seen in an earlier paragraph that this
is a good way to learn management skills. It is also
true that one of the first skills you will learn is how
to deal with management cases.

TEACHING BY CASE METHOD

INTRODUCTION TO PART II

Unless you have had considerable experience as a teacher or trainer in using cases, you will find it useful to read Part I, directed to students. In fact, even if you have had such experience, you should study that first part before assigning it to your students. If it says anything that is too far removed from your own opinion about case method you will want to call your students' attention to the difference in preference. Many styles of using cases have grown up, and there is nothing more uncomfortable for a teacher than to try to teach one way when the case is designed for another or the students expect a third. For example, to foreshadow a later definition, one difference in style involves <u>the degree of direction</u> the teacher exercises over the class discussion. The teacher who tries to be completely "non-directive" in a class of students who have not yet learned how to start a discussion on their own is bound to be frustrated, and the class will be frustrated as well.

In Part II our manual will describe various styles of using cases and various case types. The author's preferences for certain styles and types may become fairly clear. None the less, it should be emphasised of any one style of teaching or type of case. Differences in course topics, differences in student populations, differences between early and late sessions of the course and many other differences warrant different treatment. Even on the spur of the moment, if your students appear to have come to class poorly prepared to discuss a case, you will have to decide whether to direct a discussion, lecture on a related topic and reassign the case for a later discussion, or perhaps even dismiss the class as a mild form of discipline.

While allowing for individual differences in purposes for using cases and styles of teaching, there are none the less five common elements of case teaching that need to be addressed:

- conducting the case class;

- choosing and using the individual case;

- course development: choosing the sequence of cases in a course;

- evaluation and grading of student work;

- case types and purposes.

Each of these topics is the subject of a separate chapter.

CONDUCTING THE CASE CLASS

5

Much of the justification of case method as a
teaching tool rests on the idea that individual students
and the class as a group learn more readily under case
method because they accept more responsibility for the
conduct of the class discussion than in other learning
methods.   On the other hand, many teachers who start
using the case method have had extensive prior experience
only with lecturing.   It is not surprising, therefore,
that a recurring issue in case method classes is, "how
much direction should the teacher provide?".

The only satisfactory answer to this question is "it
depends" - on the teacher's purpose, on the students'
readiness to accept responsibility, on the character and
content of the case at hand and a good many other variables.   Without trying to exhaust the subject, the
following diagram, figure 3, suggests the most important
determinants of the decision.   Teaching style should be
a matter of conscious decision, not happenstance.   The
teacher continually bears the burden of judging whether
the students are learning.   In case method the teacher
has a fine opportunity to discover this by hearing and
judging the quality of students' class presentations.

Selecting the teaching style

Styles of direction vary.   Some case method
teachers routinely assign groups of students to prepare
case reports and make oral presentations as "briefings",
while the teacher sits in the audience, taking little or
no part in the performance.   Other teachers assign
individual students in rotation to direct the classes
from the front of the classroom.   These may be thought
of as extreme examples of "non-directive" teaching.   It
is clearly useful for student groups to gain experience
in making brief presentations, and the case method

Figure 3   Determinants of responsibility for direction of discussion

Variable	More teacher direction	More student direction
Time in course	Early ⟹	Late
Teacher's purpose	To illustrate a specific concept ⟹	To encourage students to develop concepts
Students' level of preparation	Students unprepared ⟹	Students well prepared
Students' stage of experience	Inexperienced students ⟹	Advanced and "post-experience" students
Nature of case	Unstructured or hidden structure ⟹	Fairly obvious structure

facilitates such role playing. By and large, however, the development of <u>individual analytical skill</u> requires more frequent participation by each student than is provided by a steady progression of group presentations.

Individual students have to direct class discussions if they are learning to become teachers or trainers. Otherwise the experience of directing a class is not especially relevant to the skills you are trying to teach.   Furthermore, you as a teacher are in an awkward position to provide feedback to other students in the class, once you completely delegate the front of the room to a student.

A third form of non-directive teaching is for the teacher to remain in the front of the classroom, but merely to call upon one volunteer student after another, interjecting no comments between recitations, venturing no opinions and asking no questions.   This technique has occasionally been used successfully with a sophisticated and experienced group of students.   The teacher can exert more control over the discussion than appears on the surface.   This control stems from non-verbal signals such as facial expression and body movement, from the choice of next speaker and from the length of time allowed to each speaker.   Most students, however, require more explicit evaluative feedback than this technique allows.   Often students believe the teacher has abdicated, and they are less willing to prepare for class unless they can expect this feedback.   Not the least of this extreme method's disadvantages is the iron self-discipline it requires of the teacher.   Using only body movements and facial expressions to control a large group of students is difficult unless the teacher is fully aware of his/her every move and its effect upon the students. It is easier and more satisfying for most of us teachers to use words to amplify our points.

At another extreme, the most directive teacher uses the day's case merely as a basis for a lecture. Students are discouraged, day after day, even from interjecting questions. The adverse effect of this technique on students' preparation before class is obvious. If you plan to be this directive, it is far better to think of not using case method.

Most effective case method teachers operate well within the extremes of style mentioned above. They use a combination of devices, some of which are described below, to keep the discussion moving, provide needed information, encourage widespread participation and give evaluative feedback. The "plot" of a case method class session might be conceived of as something like the diamond shape diagram shown as figure 4. At the beginning, the scope of the discussion is narrow, containing only the ideas of the opening speaker. As other students introduce their ideas, conflicting with or amplifying the opener as the teacher asks probing questions or seeks clarification, the matter under discussion becomes much broader in scope and far more complex.

Perhaps midway in the discussion and after about one-half to two-thirds of the class period has elapsed, a class that is "going well" will seem to start to converge, as in the bottom half of the diamond. Some competing ideas, having gained no support, will be forgotten. Other suggestions, after argument, will be explicitly set aside. Consensus will develop about objectives, certain ways of stating the problem(s) and certain alternatives that are worthy of consideration. Eventually the class will focus on one or two solutions most students are willing to accept as reasonable. In some cultures, at least, the fact that each class session is of fixed duration seems to force eveyone, students and teacher alike, towards "closure". Everyone wants to arrive at a "satisfactory" ending.

As the case method teacher you should therefore view your responsibility as facilitating this pattern. It is probably true that a class period is as unsatisfactory if the students agree too soon on a single line of argument as it is if they never get around to choosing among the welter of conflicting views. It is therefore equally important to make sure the class understands the full complexity of the case situation as it is to help them converge towards the end of the class session. As

Figure 4   Content of a case discussion over time

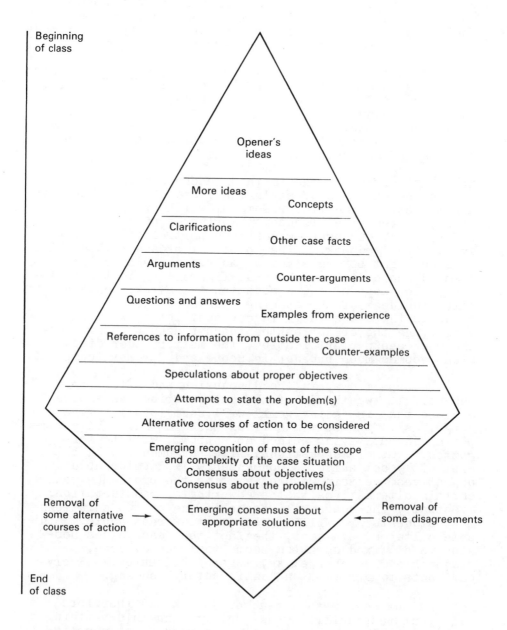

Beginning
of class

Opener's
ideas

More ideas

Concepts

Clarifications

Other case facts

Arguments

Counter-arguments

Questions and answers

Examples from experience

References to information from outside the case

Counter-examples

Speculations about proper objectives

Attempts to state the problem(s)

Alternative courses of action to be considered

Emerging recognition of most of the scope
and complexity of the case situation
Consensus about objectives
Consensus about the problem(s)

Removal of
some alternative →
courses of action

Emerging consensus about
appropriate solutions

Removal of
← some disagreements

End
of class

40

the teacher, you have a sizable number of devices, apart
from directly taking charge and lecturing, to facilitate
the process.

Useful techniques for leading case discussions

Requesting clarification of students' prior
statements.

Rephrasing what the student has said, to see if the
meaning is clear, and to assist other students in following what is being said.   There is a fine line between
true rephrasing and twisting the meaning to fit what you
believe the student should have said.   The latter is to
be avoided.

Asking probing questions that force students to
expand their arguments.   Sometimes these questions may
be in the form, "why to you recommend such a course of
action?" or "what evidence do you have that such and
such is true?".   In general your questions should be
asked in neutral, rather than antagonistic words.   There
are far more students who need encouragement to expand
their own thinking than there are those who thrive on
direct arguments with the teacher.   But some excellent
case method teachers, knowing individual students well,
make good use of the role of "devil's advocate".   That
is, they deliberately set out to represent an adversary
point of view, to put pressure on the student to probe
deeper into argument.

Interpreting and reporting illustrative experience.
At times a case contains special-purpose words or jargon
with which the students are not familiar.   This is
particularly frequent with cases written in a region
foreign to the student.   The teacher must clarify
quickly, to avoid letting the class bog down in specula-
tion about definitions.   Less frequently, a case may be
unclear on a point of fact.   Where the uncertainty is
not one of the central issues of the case, i.e. the type
of fact that would be uncertain for the manager in the
real-world situation, you as the teacher can introduce
an acceptable working assumption to get the class
started again.

Giving "lecturette": introducing concepts and
techniques.   One of the most frequently asked questions
about case method teaching is, "how do you expect
students to learn well-known concepts without your
introducing them?   Must every student reinvent the
wheel?"   The main answer to this is the "technical
note" which is described in Chapter 9, along with other

assigned auxiliary reading, both of which are integral
parts of "case method".   But every case method teacher
has experienced the need to take a short time in the
middle of a class to clarify or amplify a concept or
technique.   This might be thought of as a "lecturette".
Some case method teachers are embarrassed at using such
a device.   They need not be.   When students are ready
to receive a bit of information because it will
immediately help them to solve a problem in the case at
hand, it will take far less time to explain the new idea
than it would in a full-blown lecture.   A case in point
is this manual itself.   Although it is designed to
accompany a series of case teaching and case learning
experiences, because it is being written without an
audience present it seems necessary to develop ideas at
more length.   The author has had the experience of con-
veying nearly every idea in the manual as an almost
automatic by-product of the case teaching process itself.
That method seems far more "natural" than is the act of
writing the ideas down.

Providing evaluative feedback in words and actions.
This activity is so central to the role of the teacher
that a later chapter is devoted entirely to it.   It is
important to realise, however, that the feedback process
also influences the flow of the class discussion.   By
appearing to ignore a useful contribution or by welcom-
ing openly a frivolous statement, the teacher has an
effect on the other students as well as the speaker.

It is easy for the teacher to forget that all direct
feedback to individual students contains elements of
reward and punishment.   No matter how kindly may be
your intentions, the student may interpret your critical
remarks as deeply personal attacks.   Particularly in
cultures where it is difficult to encourage students to
recite, you should avoid direct criticism and sarcasm
in the classroom.   One way to check your own response
patterns, and to avoid making too hasty a negative response, is to ask yourself mentally, "what do I like
about the student's statement?".   If you can find
nothing you like about a recitation, it is better to call
on another student quickly without making any comment.

Writing on the chalkboard or other public recording
device.   By use of the chalkboard the teacher can
influence greatly what the class pays attention to.
Words and phrases recorded on the board tend to remain
"in" the field of discussion.   Students whose entire
recitations draw not so much as a single word recorded
on the board, on the other hand, tend to fall silent;
they believe they must not have made a useful contribution.   The board allows the teacher to "organise" what
is otherwise a somewhat incoherent presentation by

placing words in special places on the board. Often, for example, one student will be talking about "objectives"; the next will want to specify "the problem"; while a third is ready to define "alternatives". Merely by placing the records of their recitations on different parts of the chalkboard, the teacher can prepare for a later specification of headings which keep the categories straight (in terms of the problem-solving format set forth in Chapter 2). By thus being a sensitive "secretary", the teacher wields great power over the direction taken by the class discussion.

Choosing the next speaker and deciding how long a recitation is allowed to run on. Many case method teachers make a practice of calling mainly on students who indicate their interest in talking by raising their hands. Particularly in cultures where students are uncomfortable in reciting, this is especially important in the early class sessions, so that no one will need to admit openly to being unprepared for recitation. Other teachers, and all teachers at one time or another, use a "call list", which they prepared in advance, to make sure that they get inputs from students who have otherwise remained silent. What is important is to inform your students in advance what your policy will be, so that they can effectively adapt to the system.

Whatever system you use, you should be aware of two or three devices related to calling for recitation. You will soon know your students well enough so that you can foresee, within limits, what a given student's input will be at any time his/her hand is in the air. That is, some students are naturally drawn to "break new ground", others to adding and supporting the previous speaker, others to counter-argument. Some are especially likely to work with the numbers in the case, while others will rarely talk about any except the qualitative facts. You may even discover some students who can be relied on to interject a note of humour into the session. Such inputs are often needed when argument gets heated.

It is worth knowing that if you want to encourage a counter-argument you had best call on a student sitting on the other side of the room from the previous speaker, all other things being equal. If one of your students is dozing, calling in turn upon students sitting at his/ her left and right, or greatly reducing the pitch of your voice as you direct a question in that direction, often brings a student to alert attention.

Answering questions.   Often students ask case
method teachers questions which directly or indirectly
mean, "what is the approved answer to this situation?".
Almost never should you be flattered into giving a direct
answer to such questions.   Once you have given a statement, even if you qualify it as "just my own opinion",
the students will find it hard to continue their own
independent analyses and speculations.   Two good ways
to respond to direct questions are to refer the question
to the rest of the class or to direct it back at the
questioner.   Then the question is an indirect request
for your own opinion, often it is best to openly interpret it as such and refer it back again to the questioner.

Summarising.   At times the class may bog down trying to deal with excessive amounts of complexity.   This
often occurs about where the diamond in figure 4 is at
its widest.   When the class is having difficulty in
discarding ideas, the teacher can help start the process
by giving a short summary statement of the previous discussion.   At such times it may be appropriate to call
attention to the underlying "organisation" of the ideas
that you have recorded on the chalkboard, for example.

It would be a mistake, however, for you to make an
unvarying practice of interjecting a summary at this
point or any other point in the class.   Just as the
master carpenter must give the apprentice the experience
of doing every part of the job of building a house, the
case method teacher must let the students experience
every facet of the mental exercise of analysis and synthesis of problem situations.   Periodic summaries of
group progress are important parts of this process.   If
the students are led to believe that it is the teacher
who performs such summaries, they will not venture to do
it.

This is particularly true of the frequently used
summary at the end of the session.   It is the rare case
method teacher who can resist the temptation to twist
such a last-minute summary so that it "comes out right",
in terms of the teacher's preferred solution to the
case problem.   In the author's opinion it is better to
refrain from summing up at the end of the class, or to
ask some student to do the summary, than for the teacher
to make a constant practice of summarising.   Once again,
if the students come to expect a neat summary by the
teacher they will be happy to stop short of completing
the class discussion for themselves.   They will allow
the teacher to close each discussion as time grows short,
and will sometimes passively resist any other ending to
a class.   The price for giving students the opportunity
to think is often a feeling of frustration on your part

as the teacher. You will often have a sense that something has been left incomplete or untidy, but you must
resist the temptation to tidy things up yourself if you
expect your students ever to gain the skill to do it.

Pausing. That leads finally to one of the most
powerful teaching techniques available to the case
method teacher: the pause. Often what is most needed
in a class discussion is not for the teacher to rush in
to fill a short silence, but to let the silence weigh
on the class. It is appropriate to recognise that this
advice, like much of the rest of the material devoted
to teaching and learning, is subject to substantial
differences from one culture to another. A period of
silence as short as 30 seconds may seem intolerably long
to an American, while being merely a normal pause in
conversation in another culture. That is all the more
reason for you, as a teacher, to make a habit of dele-
gating to the students the responsibility for keeping
the discussion going.

In sum, the successful case method teacher must
accept a significantly different role from that of the
lecturer. Because students learning under case method
are required to prepare before class, they must be given
every possible opportunity to demonstrate their degree
of preparation. Since the total amount of time available for a case course is often about the same as that
devoted to a lecture series, the teacher must relinquish
time so that the students may present ideas. This
adjustment is often the most difficult one for the former
lecturer to make.

Preparing for a case method class

There is a temptation for teachers unfamiliar with
case method to assume that it is easier and quicker for
the teacher to prepare for a case class than for a lecture. "After all", their line of reasoning goes,
"the students do all the work". Nothing could be
farther from the truth. The author believes that it
takes more time to prepare for a case class than for a
lecture. He also believes that preparing for a case
class is more enjoyable, which makes the extra effort
worth while, but that is a matter of personal preference.
You must decide that for yourself. The reason that
case class preparation is more time consuming than preparing a lecture is that case preparation is part of an
"open system" whereas the lecture is far more often a
"closed system".

The lecturer usually is concerned with introducing ideas in one "logical" order. Having defined your field of study to your own satisfaction, as a lecturer you divide the topic into manageable pieces and introduce ideas "efficiently", in such an order as to build each upon the previous ones. Although you may experiment and re-experiment with the order of introduction of ideas, within any given syllabus period the system is reasonably closed. You will choose your real-world illustrations in such a way that they do not raise questions in students' minds about ideas and concepts you have not yet introduced. In the extreme and most rigid form of lecture method, where students are discouraged from asking questions, the system is entirely closed. Someone antagonistic to such extreme lecturers has said, "a lecture is a process whereby words pass from the lecturer's notebook to the note pads of the students, without passing through the heads of either".

By contrast, you, as a case method teacher, work in an open system. Although you will have an underlying purpose for assigning a particular case and case series (as is explained in Chapters 6 and 7), you can never be certain that all the students will find in the case what you "expect" them to find. Cases drawn from real-world situations do not come with handy labels saying, "solve this by using linear programming", or "Maslow's theory of the hierarchy of needs explains this human problem". Furthermore, in the inter-action called for by the case method class, the teacher often finds a student who is an expert in some facet of management, or who has had an illuminating experience not available to the teacher. The case method teacher, far more than the lecturer, must be prepared so as not to be threatened by the open discussion.

As a result of the complexity of cases and of the diversity which students will introduce into the class period, you as a teacher must be doubly prepared:

- you must be intimately familiar with the facts of the case and with as many as possible of the logical interpretations of those facts;

- you must have an image in your mind of one or more analytical structures that can usefully be applied to solving the case, including those with which students may not yet be familiar; yet

- you must not become so convinced of the correctness of a single solution that your mind is closed to the innovative student who approaches the case from an original point of view.

It is this open system characteristic of case method teaching which has led experienced case teachers to assert that they see something new in a case each time they use it with a new group of students, no matter how often they have used it before.

With the foregoing in mind, there are a few useful suggestions for the teacher in preparing for a case class discussion.

The first two steps are the same as for the student - a quick first reading and a careful, more thorough second reading (see Chapter 1). These readings primarily give you intimate familiarity with the case. Incidentally, if you are using a case that you yourself have written, these steps also remind you of what facts are available to the students. You, of course, will know a great deal more about the actual situation than appears in the case. You can save yourself and the students a good deal of frustration by re-analysing the situation using only the case facts; this will save you from expecting too much from the students.

The third step is different for the teacher from the third step for the students. Whereas each student will, at this point, become more and more convinced of a single "correct" solution, you should try to reason through the most convincing lines of argument for all feasible solutions, as well as the most compelling counter-arguments related to each alternative. Somewhat like the football or basketball coach who is pre-planning a match against an untested opponent, you must think through not only all manners of attack but also all possible defences.

Your fourth step is to review your reasons for the inclusion of the particular case at this point in your course. It is probably true that a spirited and well-argued case discussion can stand on its own as a learning experience, whether or not the class develops skill in the concept area you have planned for. None the less you must be able, after the class period is over, to measure how well the class performed in terms of your course timetable. It is all very well to say, "the class was interested and discussion was lively; the students must have learned something today". But if you believe that it is about time for the students to demonstrate comprehension of the difference between formal and informal organisation structures, you must be able to review the class session in conceptual terms.

One facet of case method is very "forgiving" to the teacher. Because cases come from real life, they contain a certain amount of redundancy. Thus, if a concept is not learned by discussing Case A, it may be picked up from Case B or Case E. This allows individual students to learn things at different speeds, and tends to re-inforce concepts through multiple use, after they have been learned. But you cannot rely on case redundancy to do all your work for you. If the chance to learn a concept has appeared in several cases, and is central to the case in hand, you should expect several students to use the concept, if it has been learned. If it does not appear, you may have to give a lecturette about it. You can only be prepared to introduce such structure into the class if you have thought, beforehand, about the concepts you want to see displayed during the class.

A fifth step is available to you in using some cases, for which teaching notes are available. These notes, prepared by the author of the case, suggest ways of analysing the case and/or tell you how previous groups of students have reacted to the case. Some case method teachers find such teaching notes very helpful. Others do not. It is a matter of personal preference whether or not to use a note. If you do use it, you will also have to decide whether to study it first or last in your sequence of preparation. If it is likely to become a "crutch", which prevents you from the wide-ranging study detailed in the four steps above, you should definitely plan to leave it till last, or ignore it altogether.

If there remained any doubt about the need for heavy preparation before class, it was dispelled for the author when he learned that one of his most respected teachers spent the entire day prior to each of his class sessions in preparation of the case. This, despite the fact that he had written many of the cases himself and had taught many of them several times before.

CHOOSING AND USING THE INDIVIDUAL CASE

6

Nearly every case, almost no matter how well or how poorly written in an objective sense, can be used by the teacher who wrote it.   Problems of style and missing information can be overcome by the teacher's interjecting information into the class session itself.   (The same cannot quite so easily be said if the case is used as the basis of a written assignment, however.)   When you as a teacher want to use a case written by someone else, you should pay particular attention to the topic and setting, and the contents and the style of writing. Once you have developed substantial experience in using cases, you will find that you have a useful mental library of cases to fill almost every need.   Furthermore, you will have developed preferences for cases written by particular authors.   Until that time, however, nothing will take the place of your careful reading and working through each case you plan to use, well in advance of assigning it to your students.

You can find out about the topic and the setting, and something about the contents of existing cases from a good bibliographical reference, such as that provided by the Intercollegiate Case Clearing House (ICCH).   The ICCH, about which more is said in a later chapter, is the custodian of the world's largest collection of cases in business administration.   A copy of sample bibliographical references is shown as figure 5.[1]

---

[1] Reproduced from Intercollegiate Bibliography Current Best Sellers (Boston, Mass., ICCH, 1977), pp. 28, 93 and 113.   With kind permission of the publisher.

Figure 5 Examples of bibliographical references to cases

NUMBER	TITLE	ABSTRACT	SETTING	AUTHORS	SOURCE/PAGES/TYPE	SUBJECTS
9 175 143	DRAGO CHEMICAL	FOCUSES ON THE MOST MEANINGFUL WAY TO MEASURE PERFORMANCE IN A PERIOD OF HIGH INFLATION. BOTH RETAIL PRICE ADJUSMENTS AND LIFO/FIFO INVENTORY VALUATION ARE CONSIDERED. A SUBSIDIARY ISSUE IS INTEGRATION OF EXTERNAL AND INTERNAL REPORTING.	ENGLAND, CHEMICAL, $40 MILLION SALES, 1974 MCFARLAN FW HARVARD UNIVERSITY, 10P	ACCOUNTING INVENTORY METHOD MANAGEMENT CONTROL	INFLATION INVENTORY VALUATION ENGLAND	GEN EXP
9 413 137	HARWICK, SMYTH, & BLANCHARD, INC. (A)	ISSUES OF ORGANIZING A ONE-YEAR OLD BROKERAGE FIRM FOR GROWTH. INVOLVES DELINEATING MAJOR FUNCTIONS, DESIGNING JOBS, SETTING UP COMPENSATION SYSTEM, AND DETERMINING POLICIES FOR RECRUITING AND PROMOTION.	NEW YORK, BROKERAGE, 18 EMPLOYEES, 1961 SEILER JA ALLEN SA III HARVARD UNIVERSITY, 15P	INVESTMENT BROKERS ORGANIZATIONAL DESIGN PERSONNEL ADMINISTRATION EMPLOYEE SELECTION NEW YORK	ORGANIZATIONAL BEHAVIOR EXECUTIVE COMPENSATION SECURITY MARKETS PROMOTION POLICY	FIELD
9 513 009	CHOUFONT-SALVA, INC.	THIS IS AN INTEGRATIVE MARKETING CASE THAT DEALS WITH THE PROBLEM OF POPULATION GROWTH, AN AREA THAT IS RECEIVING CRITICAL ATTENTION IN ALMOST ALL DEVELOPING ECONOMIES. THE MANAGEMENT OF CHOUFONT-SALVA, A LOCAL DRUG COMPANY, HAS DECIDED TO MARKET AN ORAL CONTRACEPTIVE IN THE PHILIPPINES. MANAGEMENT IS NOW FACED WITH THE CHALLENGE OF DEVELOPING A VIABLE MARKETING PLAN IN LIGHT OF THE MARKETING ENVIRONMENT IN THE PHILIPPINES. IN DEVELOPING A COMPREHENSIVE MARKETING PROGRAM, THE STUDENT MUST IDENTIFY THE COMPANY'S TARGET MARKET AND DECIDE UPON AN OVERALL MARKETING STRATEGY TO REACH THIS MARKET. THIS INCLUDES MAKING DECISIONS REGARDING SUCH MATTERS AS CHANNELS OF DISTRIBUTION, BRAND NAME, PACKAGING, PRICE, AND ADVERTISING AND PROMOTIONAL ACTIVITIES.	PHILIPPINES, DRUG, 1966 SORENSON RZ II FELTON EL JR IPP, 23P	PHARMACEUTICALS SALES PROGRAM MARKET RESEARCH BRANDS ADVERTISING	MARKETING MARKETING STRATEGY CHANNELS OF DISTRIBUTION PRICING PHILIPPINES	FIELD

Topic

It almost goes without saying that cases dealing
with accounting problems will be most useful in accounting courses, production area cases in production
courses, and so on.   Case bibliographies therefore are
primarily organised around "subject-area" categories.
The ICCH subject categories, identified with the second
digit of the case number, are as follows: 1 - Control
(accounting); 2 - Finance; 3 - General (policy and
planning); 4 - Human; 5 - Marketing; and 6 - Production and operations management.   These subject categories match up well with most curricula in America,
although courses which focus specifically on quantitative
methods of decision making and some specialised courses
(transportation and logistics, for example) are not
specifically served by these six major subject headings.

It is possible to determine more narrowly the focus
of a case by reference to the bibliography, however.
In the lower right-hand corner of the bibliographical
reference is shown a list of words which represent the
case author's opinions about what concepts are covered
in the case.   A substantial number of these conceptual
focus identifications are cross-indexed in the ICCH
bibliography.   For example, in the finance area, you
may be interested in cases related to capital budgeting;
this topic is shown in the "topics" index, with the case
numbers of all those cases whose authors have said that
their cases are useful in teaching capital budgeting.
In similar fashion, specialised subtopics of marketing,
such as "channels of distribution", "advertising media"
and "market research" are noted.   Also, within the
topic index, you can find references to cases that have
particular environmental settings: "inflation", "international enterprise", "small business" and "Canada" are
examples.

Contents

Once you have identified a case number that seems
to hold promise for your course, a reference to the
specific abstract (see figure 5) gives you a short description of the case situation.   Authors, unfortunately,
tend to differ markedly in the abstracts they write about
their cases.   It is most useful when the abstract des-
cribes the nature of the decision or action setting,
rather than a precis of the information given in the
case.   None the less, enough information is often giving
in the abstract to enable you to discover whether you
have further interest in the case.   Several other specifics are given, including the organisational and geographic setting of the case, the authors' names and

affiliation, the "type" of case and its length in pages. Once you have identified an author whose cases you like, you can then use the author index to find new cases, as well.

Two cases shown in figure 5 are described as "field", meaning that the authors gathered their data by visiting the organisation about which the case was written. In later chapters of this book considerable attention will be paid to the process of writing cases based upon field research. Suffice it to say that the majority of cases listed in the ICCH bibliographies are "field" cases. A few are "library" or "published data" based. Another group, of which an example is also given in figure 5, are shown as based on "generalised experience". These cases are often the inventions of authors who have wide experience in a subject-area as a a result of years of teaching and consulting in the field. If an inexperienced teacher were to write such a case, it would probably be referred to as an "armchair" case, by which is meant a case which is purely made up to present an "example" of a particular sort of decision the teacher wants to demonstrate. In a later chapter the extensive reasons for doing field research for case writing will be presented. Suffice it to say here that in selecting cases for your own use, you should make sure that any case from "generalised experience" truly contains the full amount of detail you need. Several cases written from the generalised experience of "old masters" in the teaching of business administration have survived to become "classics". Most "armchair" cases last only as long as the author uses them.

The length of the case is a seemingly trivial bit of data. None the less, it is extremely important. Although there is no single standard by which a case may be identified as "too long", "too short", or "just right", you will soon discover the limits you can safely use with your own students. Cases between 3 and 12 pages are likely to be satisfactory for teaching in almost any course, except general management and business or public policy. For these latter courses, cases tend to be slightly longer, in order to contain the variety of data necessary to introduce students to top management complexities. Cases shorter than three pages may turn out to have too few data to support careful analysis; some exceptions to this are situations that have been abstracted in quantitative terms to illustrate special mathematical techniques of analysis. Some excellent human relations cases are also very short, yet prove to be satisfactory for teaching purposes. They achieve their excellence by reminding students of similar personal experiences of their own. Thus the subject-matter for class discussion is not so much the case facts as it is the individual experiences of the students.

One other type of information is contained in some bibliographical references to cases. When the author has provided a "teaching note", or when a case is a part of a series of cases that should be used in a particular sequence, this information will be shown. Many case method teachers find it more comfortable to use cases written by others when the authors have provided teaching notes. The teaching notes are, of course, made available by a clearing-house only to teachers and trainers.

The ICCH and other case clearing organisations and case libraries growing up around the world[1] make cases available to teachers and trainers at modest cost. They do not attempt to judge whether cases are effective or ineffective, although they do usually ask authors not to submit cases until the cases have been tested in the classroom and rewritten if necessary. Furthermore, if a case appears in the bibliography volume "Current Best Sellers", it demonstrates that the case has stood the test of time and market acceptance. None the less, every teacher bears the final responsibility for choosing appropriate cases. Although bibliographies and recommendations by other teachers can call your attention to a case, only by reading it and working it out for yourself can you determine whether it fits your purposes. This is true of topic, setting and contents. It is even more true of style.

Style

A later section of this book will deal in some detail with the question of style, from the point of view of the case writer. The same ideas are pertinent to the teacher who is selecting a case. They are summarised here for convenience.

The most important element of style is for case facts to be reported at the lowest possible level of abstraction. By this is meant that the facts as given in the case should be devoid, as much as possible, of the case writer's opinion about relationships of cause and effect among the facts as reported. A central justification of case method is that it allows students to develop skill in problem solving. As Chapter 2 has

---

[1] See Appendix 15.

pointed out, a critical part of solving problems is to be able to analyse cause and effect relationships among facts in the past and present situations, and to predict consequences of today's actions in the future.   If a case writer asserts cause and effect relationships in the very style of writing the case itself, students are unlikely to probe to discover the relationships for themselves.   You can protect your students against having to experience the frustration of "analysing" a case which the case writer has already partially solved, by being extremely sensitive to writing style.   In the most blatant instances, case writers may write sentences such as, "the business had been losing money because of a decline in sales and an increase in operating costs". Any uses of the words "because" or "cause" or "effect" suggest that the case writer may have overstepped the bounds.   What you must ask yourself is whether the case still leaves open for the student to discover enough to serve your teaching purposes.

A more subtle form of pre-analysis of a case by the case writer is the selection of facts in such a way as to bias the analysis.   There is no easy clue for you to discover this without your own careful study of the case.   One indication that such a bias might be present is for the facts of a case to appear to come from just a single source, usually one manager.   It is true that a great many excellent cases are written from the view- point of just one manager;   in instances where few human relations are involved in the case this is not particularly damaging.   But in human behaviour cases, and particularly in situations where the single- information-source manager is deeply involved in a con- flict, his or her information is likely to be biased. When the case writer is a central figure in the case situation, bias is almost impossible to avoid.

Good case writers will make liberal use of quota- tions and attributions of opinion to case characters if they find that principals in the case have a biased viewpoint or may already have come to some conclusions about cause and effect relationships.   As was pointed out in an earlier chapter, opinions of case characters are "open to challenge" by the student, as a matter of case method convention.

Another subtle method of pre-analysing the case is the use of special "jargon".   When a psychiatrist says that someone is suffering from an "Oedipus complex", students of psychology have an entire framework of expectations, based upon their previous study of such cases.   The effective use of jargon is very important in saving time and words in discussing well-diagnosed situations.   As a teacher you would probably like to

54

see your students develop a rich special-purpose vocabulary related to your field of study. When a case makes excessive use of jargon, however, it tends to shut off the discovery process for the students. If it were a central purpose of a teacher of psychiatry to teach students how to diagnose "Oedipus complex" in a patient, you can be sure that the description of the situation would not include those words, but would concentrate on more detailed symptoms. Usually we develop special-purpose words to summarise situations about which we have learned something useful in general. The student (or manager) who has learned to identify a number of facts occurring together as symptoms of some condition that can be summarised by a jargon phrase is in a position, thereafter, to design effective actions. As a teacher, therefore, you should get in the habit of recognising jargon wherever it appears in cases. Once again, the critical question for you to answer is, "after the student has been given all the assistance provided by the jargon in the case, is there enough analysis left to be done, to serve my purposes in using this case?".

You will frequently have to choose among cases each of which shows flaws to some extent. Case writing is not a perfected science, and no case writer can be sufficiently aware of his/her own prejudices to avoid them completely. There is one other type of flaw, however, which should lead you not to use a case under any circumstances. This is a case in which the writer's own value system is obvious. In effect, in such cases, the case writer is saying to the student, "not only have I told you what causes were producing the effects I observed, but I also want you to know just what effects are desirable and which are undesirable". Once again, it is permissible for the case writer to report the values of case characters, but not to write them in as absolutes which cannot be challenged by the student. It is particularly dangerous for case writers from one culture to write cases about another culture and to include their own value systems as part of the case.

As a teacher you will not find it difficult to identify the most blatant instances of value judgements by the case writer. It is particularly true that you will find it easy to avoid using cases where the case writer's value judgements are different from yours. It is much more difficult for you to avoid cases written by case writers whose value systems are similar to yours, and where the value judgements are buried in the case. What you must be alert to, in choosing cases, is every hint of judgements about what is "good" or "bad". Such judgements often appear in the case writer's choice of adjectives. As an example, the statement, "a film of road dust covered the hotel-keeper's desk" is a statement of fact. "The hotel-keeper's desk was filthy with road dust" shows the case writer's value judgement about dust. The first statement leaves open for the students to judge, whereas the latter statement is sure to prejudice the students in the analyses of the case. Whether or not you tend to agree with the case writer's judgements, those judgements do not belong in the case. They inhibit the student's development of judgement processes.

Before leaving this question of case style, it may be well to emphasise that the author believes that case method teachers have a great deal of responsibility for helping students to develop value systems and effective ways to think about "good and bad". (Although, for the practical manager, the words "good and bad" might often be replaced by "effective and ineffective".) But the way for the teacher to do this is in classroom interaction with students, not by inserting the value judgements in cases, or allowing them to be inserted in cases by unknown case writers.

Mechanics of use of the single case

Case method requires somewhat more preplanning on the part of the teacher than does the lecture method. If you have a last-minute thought about a lecture the night before you are to deliver it, you can merely change your notes and change your message. Cases must be in the students' hands long enough before the class for them to prepare for the discussion. If you are requiring a written paper you may want them to have even more than usual time for preparation.

When cases appear in published case books, and each student has a copy of the case book, the problem of case availability and consistency becomes quite easy. It still is necessary for you to determine whether the case is free from damaging errors. Particularly in the instance of a first edition of a case book, substantial errors can creep into the case. Sometimes the numbers in one table will not agree with similar numbers in another table. Sometimes textual references to quantities will not reconcile with the same quantities at their source in exhibits. Within the text itself, sometimes phrases or sentences are left out, which makes it impossible to know exactly what is meant. When such problems arise in cases, it is your responsibility as a teacher to identify them in advance, call them to your students' attention, and give the students a working assumption about what the "true" case fact should be.

56

When you have finished using a case book for the first time, of course, it is courteous to write the authors about changes that should be made in a future edition.

The problems in the use of loose-leaf cases, such as are provided by ICCH and other case libraries, are similar, but compounded by other difficulties as well. Although loose-leaf cases are copyrighted and are not supposed to be copied by others, it is none the less true, particularly in international extension of case use, that loose-leaf cases are often copied without permission of the authors or the library. When such copies are made photographically, no additional typographical errors are introduced. But in many instances the copier finds it cheaper to retype a case on mimeograph masters. In such instances the number of typographical errors increases enormously. The author has had the experience of teaching in circumstances where his copy of the case differed in substantial details from the copies being used by the students. It is not infrequent for there to be several "versions" of the same case in the files of a management institution, without any way to be sure which version is which without reading it word for word. Some advice for institutions who use loose-leaf cases or establish case libraries is included in a later chapter. The individual teacher can only do as much as possible to protect students against the disappointment of typographical flaws in the cases as they are used.

Lest the foregoing warnings sound as if the use of loose-leaf cases is more trouble than it is worth, it is well to point out the major advantage of using loose-leaf cases, which is flexibility. If you have a "series" case, in which several separate situations involving the same company have been written, you can issue each case to the students in just the sequence you want. When such cases are printed in published case books, each subsequent case is "open" to the student who reads ahead of the assignment schedule. If you plan to use a loose-leaf case as the basis for a test or a written assignment, you can issue it just when you want the students to start work on the case, rather than to hope that none of the students will have been working ahead in the book in hopes of gaining advantage over others.

Finally, if you use loose-leaf cases you will find it challenging to write cases yourself to assist you in designing the course just exactly as you want it designed. "Course development", or the selection of a sequence of cases to present ideas in an effective order, is the subject of the next chapter.

COURSE DEVELOPMENT: CHOOSING THE SEQUENCE OF CASES IN A COURSE

7

There may have been a time in the evolution of case method teaching when it was considered satisfactory to teach case after case, with little attention being paid to the order in which the cases were used. If that were true, even those early case teachers would have had to choose which cases to use, out of the many available. Nowadays there are said to be tens of thousands of cases available in case libraries, and many more are being written every year. It is clearly necessary to have a process and criteria for choosing which cases to use. Furthermore, as each branch of management or administration becomes more systematised, as we develop more and better theories of how things work, it becomes all the more important to devise comfortable sequences of cases to improve the students' learning experiences.

Order of introduction of ideas

A first step in setting up a sequence of cases is to identify an appropriate order to introduce the course ideas. It may help for you to think in terms of an analogy to the building of a stone wall. The stone mason knows that he must place his layers of stones from the bottom up, building upon some solid foundation. In somewhat analogous fashion, you would build your course from the "bottom up", paying particular attention to when the students are ready for each new idea you introduce.

It is at this point that the stone wall analogy becomes a little too simple. The stone mason has a right to expect that the concrete foundation will be reasonably flat and level, and that a good quality of cement will have been used, so that each part of the foundation will bear the weight of the stones laid upon it. Every experienced teacher knows that the "foundations" of students vary in level and in quality of preparation. It often takes several weeks of observing and testing students for the teacher to appraise the preparation each student brings to the course. A second difference is that stone masons have an easy job of selecting which stone to lay next. So long as it is solid, any stone can be laid wherever it "fits" in terms of size and shape. Cases differ not only in size (length) and shape (topic), but also in "mass" (number of new ideas and concepts per case). Deciding whether a case "fits" involves judging whether the ideas needed to analyse the case are already in the students' hands, and whether the new ideas to be gained by studying the present case are appropriate to "support" the cases which are to follow.

Undoubtedly the question of what is an effective order of introduction of ideas is an important one for a lecturer, as well as for a case method teacher. However, the sequencing of ideas may not be as highly critical to the success of a lecture series. Until the students are asked to demonstrate their skill with the use of inter-related concepts, ideas or techniques, the ideas themselves can exist in somewhat "logic-tight" compartments. It is conceivable that a student might be able easily to memorise 50 individual definitions of terms learned in lectures, without ever learning how to put the terms together into a workable basis for problem solving. Since case method gives virtually no rewards for memorising definitions, the sequencing of ideas is critical.

It is difficult to discuss the concept of "effective" sequencing in the abstract. No doubt, two equally effective case method teachers would have some differences of opinion over what was the most effective order of introducing the ideas of their courses. It is an excellent exercise for teachers who bear joint responsibility for a course to get together to discuss which ideas should come "first".

In addition, it is necessary to consider the "foundation level" or the level of "common sense". By whatever name this level is called, it emphasises the importance of specifying what it is you as a teacher expect your students to know when they arrive for the first day of your course. Unless you specify this either explicitly or implicity, you have no basis for deciding where to begin. If you expect too little common sense of your students, you will bore them by introducing ideas with which they are already familiar. If you expect too much, you risk starting in well above their level of preparation, and thus making them continue to have to ask extra questions, perhaps never to catch up.

Among the basic building blocks of every course are the definitions of specialised terms and the conventional ways of putting the simplest terms together. Perhaps it is easiest to give examples of this basic level from the field of accounting. Among the earliest specialised ideas the new student of accounting needs to learn are definitions of such simple concepts as "price", "cost" and "profit". Despite these words being part of the everyday vocabulary of practising managers and even of beginning students, in many classes there are persons who confuse "price" with "cost". In any event, among the early ideas which must be introduced to accounting students are the definitions of terms as they will be used in the course. One may well distribute a list of common definitions to the students. Operational definitions, i.e. those arrived at by "seeing the general terms in operation" are also to be provided if they are to be used in discussing a particular case.

In addition to basic ideas and definitions there are certain "conventions", which also need to be learned early in a course. The format in which a balance sheet is organised and presented is an example of such convention. The fact that British accountants prefer one format and the French ones another is a clear indication that there can be no "right" or "wrong" about the matter; it is just that people have agreed for convenience to present data in a specially organised format.

Definitions and conventions are not the only basic ideas in courses, yet they constitute a large body of material, and often take up a great deal of the time in lectures and textbooks. They also are needed before one can fully understand the analytical techniques and models. Accounting students must grasp the difference between "cost" and "price" before they can progress to an understanding of the difference between fixed and variable costs. If students are to cope with "break-even analysis" or other models dealing with "price, cost and volume relationships", they must have understood the nature of fixed and variable costs. On the other hand, a simple case involving the break-even point for a one-product firm may provide an excellent vehicle for giving the students an effective "operational definition" of fixed and variable costs. If you remain completely aware of the stage of understanding reached by your students, you can decide whether or not a particular case "fits" your syllabus at any point.

A higher level of ideas, or analytical techniques and models, concerns the "cause and effect relationships". A definition of a term or a conventional way of presenting data, no matter how complex the term or the resulting table, says nothing about cause and effect. One must bring some additional analysis to bear to draw inferences about cause and effect from data or information. Most theories deal with cause and effects. To the extent, therefore, that we wish to introduce our students to theories of management, we must move them beyond and above the stage of definitions and conventions.

There is still a higher plane in a "course pyramid", however. That is the plane of criteria for decision making, or the place where judgement is called for. This plane deals with ideas of relative value. If a single criterion is enough, and can be stated in monetary terms, this capstone level may be fairly easy to teach and fairly easy for the students to use. For example, for many years accountants have defined their decision criteria in terms of monetary profits: "The goal of management should be to maximise the long-term wealth of the shareholder." Although it may not always be easy to predict the consequences of every action upon the "long-term wealth of the shareholder", none the less this goal is an unequivocal one. Furthermore, most of our effective problem-solving models and formulae have been developed by researchers who have adopted a single monetary criterion for choice.

It should come as no surprise that we as teachers are often confronted by multiple criteria for decision making, these days, just as the managers in the real world are finding criteria more and more complex and multidimensional. This is true both in public management and in the private sector. It is for this reason that the concept of criteria for decision making occupies the top level of the course pyramid. These ideas may not necessarily be introduced last, but a complete understanding of criteria may be thought of as the capstone achievement of the successful participant in your programme.

Identifying cases with concepts

So far this chapter has paid little attention to the problem of identifying cases and technical notes that will accomplish what you want, in terms of the order of introduction of ideas and concepts in your course. As you continue to use the case method, you will develop your own personal library of favourite cases. You will identify each with the concepts you believe students can learn from discussing it. You will also continue to recognise those places in your course where you know of no case that fits well. In the short run you can fill those empty places with technical notes, readings and lectures. You can ask colleagues to recommend cases they have found effective.   In the long run, you can do the field research needed to write cases yourself.

When you are just starting to teach by cases, however, you will not yet have a personal reference file of cases, but only a list of concepts in order of planned introduction.   There is no easy short cut to develop the case list, except to adopt a published case book, in which the author has placed cases in a preplanned order. This expedient is a good one for many teachers in countries where good case books are readily available and cases are mostly drawn from the same geographical region as the students.   Even for the teacher in another culture, a careful study of established case books and their order of introduction of ideas is a very useful activity.   A list of case books is included in the bibliography of this book, so that new teachers can refer to case books in their own study fields.   As we will discover in the next chapters, not all cases are so "culture-bound" that they cannot be used in other countries to good effect.   Thus you may find in case books cases that you would like to use in your own courses. Furthermore, even if you believe that a case in a case book is too "foreign" for your students, the structure of the case may well suggest the dimensions of a case you would like to write about an organisation in your own country.

An additional activity that you should carry out is the bibliographical reference work described in Chapter 6. In order to keep track of cases to which you have been exposed, you will no doubt want to devise a filing scheme of your own.   One such scheme is the following:

Record on a file card at least the following information about each case you want to keep track of: case name, author and source;   topic (subject-area);   student concept-inputs required;   and concepts students can learn from the case.   Make enough duplicates of the cards so that you can keep one file in alphabetical order by case name, one in the order of concepts required and one in the order of concepts students can learn.

The last two items on the list above are critical for you to be able to position each case in your course. Unless you make a conscious effort to abstract cases in these terms, you will find yourself forgetting details about cases.   It is not enough to think to yourself, "that is a good case;   I must remember it".   What is a "good case" for one point in a course may be a very poor one if it is introduced so early that students lack the groundwork needed, or so late that it has nothing novel to contribute.

No record merely of what you think a case is about is sufficient, however.   Each time you use a case you should record your impressions of how well it worked in terms of your purposes.   For new cases you have written, this record will lead to revisions in the case.   For cases others have written, this post-class record will influence whether you will use the case again, where you will place it, and your classroom strategy for using it.

EVALUATING STUDENTS' WORK

8

The point has been made in earlier chapters that the case method teacher has a special responsibility to give evaluative feedback to students. The special nature of the responsibility arises because case method requires students to use judgement and make decisions. There are no "right" or "wrong" judgements in most situations. The real-world manager gets his evaluative feedback from the outcomes of his decisions. Lacking real-world outcomes, the case method students must get their feedback from your opinion of their ideas. This feedback has several forms:

- immediate response to class participation;

- written comments on students' papers;

- consultations with individual students;

- formal course grades.

Immediate response to class participation

As was mentioned in Chapter 5, your response to a student's recitation in class affects the whole thrust of the class discussion. It is the author's opinion that direct critical feedback from the teacher in the presence of other students is very damaging to the student who receives it, and should therefore be avoided. Yet, if a student's obviously frivolous comment seems to gain favourable attention from the teacher, other students may be confused about the value of the input. Even an inept, yet well-intentioned recitation may threaten to throw the class off the trail, if you reward the student for trying. At the other extreme, your overly enthusiastic reception of a "good" idea may shut down thinking by other students.

If they believe that one student has "solved" the case, the rest of the class may quit putting forward conflicting ideas.

Faced with this dilemma, most case method teachers treat classroom evaluative feedback as primarily a matter of class direction tactics. In other words, the teacher's responses in the classroom are more determined by their expected effect on the whole class than on the individual student, except that no directly derogatory response should be made to an individual.

This then means that encouragement for useful recitations is a feasible tactic. Favourable feedback should stop short of any implication that what the student recommends is "correct" or a final word on the subject. Encouragement can be signalled by smiling and nodding as you listen to a student's words, by leaning forward towards the student who is reciting or by recording words and phrases from the recitation on the chalkboard. Verbal responses such as "I understand" or "yes; go on" will serve to keep the recitation flowing. Merely paying strict attention to one student for a longer-than-average recitation serves to reward a useful input. You should avoid long questions as part of the feedback to a student who is making a useful recitation.

Your reaction to a set of ideas you believe are without merit should be much the opposite. Record little or none of the recitation on the chalkboard. Remain silent and motionless as you hear the student's statement. Call on another student in a rather shorter-than-average time. All of these devices will serve to signal to the reciting student that you are not favourably impressed about what is being said.

Sometimes you may believe that a student, despite all your neutral yet mildly discouraging feedback, is likely to persuade the class of a viewpoint you believe is disfunctional. This may happen when the reciting student is especially glib or of such high status in the class that no other participant cares to volunteer an immediate challenge. The temptation is for you to argue the other side of the case against such a student. This is usually not the best strategy. It is better for you to devise a series of questions that will lead the student to discover the inconsistencies in his/her own argument. The outcome of such a successful exchange is likely to be better understood both by the student involved and by the class, and it avoids putting your status and that of the student directly in conflict.

The foregoing paragraphs make the explicit assumption that you are immediately aware of the quality of

each student's recitation. An implicit assumption is
that you, the teacher, bear all the responsibility for
feedback. Neither of these assumptions holds true all
the time. Often you cannot be sure whether a student's
recitation holds promise until you have heard a good deal
of it. An outstanding feature of case method is the
fact that a case situation may have several satisfactory
"solutions", depending on different lines of reasoning.
You will need, therefore, to exercise considerable self-
discipline not to cut short any recitation before being
sure you understand the thrust of the argument.

Furthermore, if you intervene too quickly to shut
down a recitation, you foreclose the feedback action of
the other students. A good class develops the habit of
general discussion, rather than merely a series of
student-teacher interchanges. To allow this pattern to
develop you must allow other students ample opportunity
to respond to a student's recitation.

Written comments on students' papers

Written comments on students' papers differ markedly
in several dimensions from open classroom feedback.
Placing comments on student papers is a private form of
feedback, with no expected effect on the rest of the
class. This is true even in cultures where it is
customary for students to show their graded papers to
their close friends. A second difference is that written comments can be designed at leisure, after you have
studied the student's entire argument. A final difference is that there is no one but you who can write comments of a student's paper. If you do not give the
feedback, it will not be done.

All of these elements of difference serve to make
written feedback on students' papers a very critical part
of the job of evaluation. Most of your teaching of the
individual student is accomplished through written feedback. Written feedback can usefully have negative as
well as positive implications. None the less, the form
and style of comments can have an important effect on the
sutdent's motivation to learn from the comments. Once
again, how you say something may be more important than
what you say.

Forms of written feedback. Written feedback consists largely of two forms, marginal notations and
general comments. Marginal notations are short statements written in the margins of the student's paper,
close to the point you wish to emphasise. General comments are summary statements giving your over-all

impression and evaluation of the paper. General comments are often written on a separate sheet of paper, attached to the student's paper when you return it.

Marginal notations are of several sorts. Frequently they call attention to a sentence or section of a student's report whose meaning is not clear to you. In such instances, there is a temptation to write a big question mark (?) in the margin, or to ask the rhetorical question "What do you mean?". The author believes that questions should be avoided in marginal notations. It is frustrating to the student to be asked a question in such circumstances, since there is no way to answer. It is better merely to make the statement, "you have not made this point clear". Even better yet is to note, "your point here would have been clearer if you had referred to an example, such as ..... in the case". Your marginal notations should signal to the student that you are paying strict attention to the message. The more you can demonstrate that you have understood of what the student is saying, the more receptive he/she will be to your suggestions for improvement.

In some marginal notations you will be signalling approval. Although there is rarely a student who will be disappointed if you write "GOOD!" in a margin, it is even better for you to say, for example, "good use of a case example here", so that the student is clear about what is being rewarded.

Other marginal notations will call attention to actual errors in logic or arithmetic. Where possible, these notes also should be complete, indicating not only where you found the error, but the nature of the error and the answer you believe is more correct. As it may be seen, the thrust of all these statements about marginal notations is in favour of their standing alone as communications. Since the student is not before you to answer questions or to ask you for clarification of your statement, you must try your best to make your statement fully understandable. If you find a great many "mistakes", whether they are in grammar, spelling or logic, you may want to ask the student to come to your office so that the matters can be worked out in more detail than is easy to do in the margins of the paper.

General comments. General comments should be something more than merely a repetition of the major marginal notations. There is a temptation to use the general comment as a thinly disguised justification for the grade you have placed on the paper. The ideal general comment will make clear to the student the class of actions he/she needs to take to improve future papers. Rarely will you find it useful to have a student redo a paper on the

same case. The skill you need to write effective
general comments is the skill of abstraction, that is to
make a statement which organises the many smaller comments in the margins.

Although there is no general formula for writing
general comments, often it is useful to return to the
problem-solving format (Chapter 2), and to refer to the
various segments of the student's paper in the terms of
the format. For example you might say, "your argument
was internally consistent, given the objective you put
forward on page ... However, page .. of the case suggests several other possible objectives. Since you
neither adopted nor specifically denied the validity of
those other objectives, I am left somewhat unconvinced
that your proposed solution is broad enough to serve the
XYZ Company's needs. Given that you have demonstrated
your skill in developing arguments from the stage of
objectives through choice of alternatives, you should
concentrate in future papers on the development of
objectives. This may require you to spend somewhat more
time in analysing the case itself, before starting into
the next steps of your work."

Consultations with individual
students

Case method both requires and facilitates consultations with individual students, to the extent your
schedule permits. It requires such consultations
because you are continually telling the students that
there is no "correct" solution to cases, and that leaves
many students anxious to have you give them additional
feedback concerning their own ideas. It facilitates
such sessions because it provides case material as a
basis for your discussion in the office. In other
words, the student is not asking you in general terms,
"how do you like my ideas?". Rather, he/she is saying,
"how can my ideas about the XYZ Company case be
improved?". You will usually find it much easier to
discuss questions like the latter than the former, the
author believes.

In the privacy of your office, faced with a single
student, you may well be tempted to forget the enormous
gulf that exists between most teachers and their students.
This gulf gives the teacher the power to hurt feelings by
overly critical statements. Even though you may believe
that what you are saying is, "your reasoning in the XYZ
case was faulty", what the student may be hearing is
"you don't know how to think!". Once again, therefore,
it is extremely important that feedback be couched in
terms of "these are ways in which your argument could be

improved, clarified and made more persuasive", rather
than "these are the ways your thinking has gone wrong".

In some cultures the process of personal consultations between teacher and student is so painful for the
student that almost any discussion becomes a punishment.
In other cultures students welcome any personal attention, interpreting it as a reward, no matter how critical
may be the message. You will have to adapt your own
styles to the cultural norms of your teaching site. Case
method can facilitate consultation where it is possible
at all, but it will not easily overturn a cultural stereo-
type against consultation.

Formal course grades

In most places where case method is used in schools
or universities the teacher is expected to give a formal
grade at the end of the course. In management training
courses and seminars the formal grade is much less
important than is a certificate of completion which
shows that the participant has diligently pursued the
course. The following remarks apply to situations where
formal grades are required.

It is quite difficult to give numerical grades (i.e.
96, 72, 85, etc.) to case method performances. Such
numerical grades suggest "objective" testing, where it is
possible to assert that a particular answer is "right" or
"wrong". None the less, it is perfectly possible to
grade case method recitations and/or written exercises
against a relative scale, saying, "this paper is better
than that one, while being less effective than a third".
Almost always you will establish your grading criteria by
a combination of a priori reasoning and a posteriori
comparisons among the students in the group.

A priori reasoning enters in in two ways. The
first way is in your expectations about a particular
case. You will have said to yourself, and written into
your grading guidelines for the exercises, "a minimum
satisfactory paper will contain specific evidence that
the student understands the notion of fixed and variable
costs. A highly satisfactory paper will use some form
of cost-price-volume modelling to decide whether or not
to undertake the new venture". You may include other
provisions for ways in which you expect students to present ideas, as well. Particularly if you have used the
case in hand with other student groups at the same level
of learning, your a priori expectations can often give
you an excellent basis for grading, without your having
to specify in advance a right answer to the case.

A posteriori qualifications come in, also. It will usually not be too difficult to identify the very best one or two papers. If these "best" papers have taken a different tack from what you had previously anticipated, you may want to modify your expectations for the class as a whole. Sometimes the present group of students will have reached a higher plane of general understanding than you had expected, sometimes a lesser plane. It is appropriate for that fact to influence the general level of grades you give. Some teachers use a "curve", by which is meant that they grade all papers on a relative scale, and then set the letter grades (A, B, C, etc.) in such a way that the mid-range of students receive mid-range grades. The author believes that case method grading can be accommodated to any desirable grading scheme except for that of assigning numbers from 0 to 100.

Types of graded work. The foregoing has dealt with graded work in terms of written papers. The author believes that most of each student's formal grade should be assigned to his/her individual written work, whether it is written homework or case analysis examinations. However, some part of the formal grade should also be given for the student's participation in class. In a curriculum where all courses are being taught by case method (which is true at only a few universities), as much as 25% of a course grade can be assessed against class participation. Instances where this percentage has been as high as 50% are not unheard of but this high a percentage may cause difficulty in interpretation. The author has given weights of 10 or 15% to class participation in case method course taught in universities where most other courses were taught by lecture method.

Class participation grades call for a scheme for keeping track of each student's participation in class. You will find it very easy to keep track of those few students who regularly take part in class, and at a very high standard. If you have more than about 15 students in the class, however, you should develop a systematic way of keeping track of every student's class participation for grading purposes. One way to do this is to have a seating chart, which requires students to sit in the same seats each day. At the end of each class period, you should then set aside a few minutes to review the class discussion, identifying on your seating chart each student who made a significant contribution, and giving a letter grade for that recitation. You will need to set some minimum number of recitations for a student to qualify for receiving a class participation grade. You will also have to make some provision, in your plan for calling upon sutdents, to encourage the silent students to participate. It will not be perceived by the students as fair treatment for you to grade silence as a zero, unless you try to have every student make enough recitations to qualify for a grade.

One variant of class participation grading that is worth considering, if you are teaching the only case method course at an institution, is to reward class participation without punishing silence. You can do this by giving a grade for participation to those students who do so, while resting the entire formal grade for those students who remain silent upon their written work.

Whatever formal grading system you use, there may be students who protest their grades. Sometimes two students will bring their papers to you, pointing out that similar ideas in the two papers drew different types of comments from you, and asking you to justify the differences in grades. It is part of the skill of case method teaching which can only be learned by experience, to be able to avoid hard feelings associated with grading. The author has found that it is possible to insist that he will always be prepared to discuss "how a student's paper can be improved", but not the level of a grade. The more you can focus the students' attention upon their responsibility for learning, the less important the grade will be as a focal point for dispute.

It should hardly need to be added that it is almost impossible for you, as a case method teacher to delegate the responsibility for grading to someone else. Although the author has had good results from having an assistant go over student papers first, to note and comment on the student's work, it has always been necessary to take final responsibility for the grades himself.

CASE TYPES AND PURPOSES

9

Most cases referred to in previous chapters are of the most common type, those which focus on a problem or a decision that needs to be made. Not all cases are of this type. Furthermore, there are other written materials that are useful in case method courses which also need to be introduced. The aim of this chapter is to introduce several types of cases and notes and to give a brief explanation of the purposes and uses of each. These are:

- problem or decision cases;

- appraisal cases;

- case histories;

- notes to accompany cases.[1]

Throughout the discussion of various case types runs a thread of the source of a case, either field research, generalised experience, library or published material. The source of material influences greatly the type of case that can be written.

---

[1] There are some other types of cases, such as the in-basket (in-tray) case or exercise and the critical incident case. They are not discussed in this work and the reader may refer to other publications, e.g. ILO: In-basket exercises for management development (Geneva, International Labour Office, 1968) and P. and F. Pigors: Case method in human relations: the incident process (New York, McGraw-Hill, 1961).

Problem or decision cases

The most frequent case type is the problem or decision case. This is a description of a situation that stops short of some decision to be made or some action to be taken. It contains, however, the facts and circumstances faced by the manager who must make the decision. Such a case brings students face to face with situations requiring decisions and actions. Using such cases they can practice the skills of analysing situations, making decisions based upon their judgement about what would be the outcomes of various courses of action, and planning the actions they will take. Because such cases have been the focus of most of the material in previous chapters, no more will be said about form and purpose of problem cases.

It is worth noting, however, that such cases must almost always be prepared either from field research or from generalised experience, and not from library research or published sources. The reason for this is that it is essential for students to have access to many sorts of information that can only come from the files of particular organisations. No manager is forced to make decisions based solely upon published documents, and it is artificial to suggest that students can learn problem solving by studying the published record, no matter how complete, of a decision that has been made by someone in the past.

The foregoing is not meant to suggest, of course, that the case must contain every scrap of information available to the manager in the real-world situation. This would be inordinately expensive, both in money and in students' time. Furthermore, experience has shown that students gain sufficient experience in selecting facts from the restricted facts available in good cases, without being flooded with the many more facts that the manager would have at hand. Even the manager in the real world often must act before he/she has all the information that would be desirable. One exercise that is often useful for students is to develop a list of the additional information they would like to have before making a final decision in a case. If they are then asked to make an estimate of the cost in time and money of getting together the additional information, they will gain a deeper understanding of the relationship between information and decisions.

Appraisal cases

Another important type of case might be called appraisal cases. The purpose of such cases is to teach students primarily the skills of analysis or appraisal of situations, short of making decisions and/or recommendations for action. There are two major types of appraisal cases: those which focus on facts inside the organisation (which might be called "micro-appraisal") and those which focus on environmental facts (which might be called "macro-appraisal" cases).

Micro-appraisal cases are often developed for use in human behaviour courses. Their purpose is to aid students in learning how to answer the question, "what is going on here?" in such terms as may be useful later on in determining a course of action to change things. In fact, it is often possible to change an appraisal case into a problem case merely by inserting a case character who is in a managerial position of responsibility. For example, an appraisal case may consist of the record of a conversation between two co-workers. The conversation may cover several pages; it would support the teacher's purpose to give students experience in using some form of analysis of inter-action. The case may provide more than enough material to occupy an entire class period, without pressing for any conclusions about what should be done. If the teacher found that the class had reached an adequate depth of understanding of the situation, while still some time remained of the class period, he/she could insert a decision maker. "Suppose that you are the superior manager to the two co-workers we have observed here, and that you had overheard this conversation. What actions would you take?"

One of the reasons that appraisal cases do not more often contain a decision-making character is that managers in the real world do not often overhear the kinds of conversations that teachers want students to know about. Such conversations may be available to case writers or consultants, but not to management people. This may be why some of the better decision-related cases in the human behaviour field are written from "generalised experience", rather than from the field.

Appraisal cases can be written about nearly every function of organisation. What characterises them in general is that the material presented stops short of that needed for making decisions, while providing ample material for answering questions like "what is going on here?". Often you can identify an appraisal case because it lacks a case character with responsibility to act in the situation.

Macro-appraisal cases have to do largely with analysing and assimilating the environment. Sometimes such cases are called "issue" cases. A description of

the circumstances surrounding an oil spill; a careful
selection of published materials about a public protest
over a nuclear power plant; excerpts from the records
of a legal battle between two giant corporations; these
are all examples of such cases. What they have in
common is a wealth of material about the environment of
an organisation. What they generally lack is comparable depth of material from inside the organisation
which would make them into full-scale problem or decision cases. Macro-appraisal cases are very frequently
written from library or published document sources. In
fact it is highly likely that any case written from such
sources should be defined as an appraisal case. It is
usually very difficult to use cases from such sources in
any other way.

One of the reasons that macro-appraisal cases
exist is that there may be almost no other way to bring
new environmental or public policy issues into the
classroom as cases. Companies who are involved in
litigation over employment practices, for example, may
be unwilling to share their inside data with a case
writer. Yet if case method teachers and case writers
were to avoid exposing their students to the new constraints and opportunities in the environment for lack
of cases, they would consign themselves to preparing
their students only for "yesterday's problems".
Furthermore, imaginative case writers do a remarkable
job of inserting individual firms' financial data into
macro-appraisal cases, from published annual reports and
other material that is in the public domain.

Case histories

Case histories have much in common with both problem and appraisal cases, while differing from both.
Frequently they may be written from field research, with
the full co-operation of the firm involved. Often, too,
they contain a good deal of environmental information,
gathered from published sources. What distinguishes
them from problem cases is that they go beyond the decision point of any relevant problem and give the decision
and its rationale. Often they also report eventual
results of the decisions. The underlying purpose of
many writers of case histories seems to be for students
to learn how a particular organisation made a successful
or unsuccessful decision. Particularly when the case
history is one of success, it is also likely that one
reason the subject organisation co-operated was to make
public the record of its success.

The author finds case histories difficult to use in
the regular run of management courses because they are

finished stories. Some universities offer courses in
business history and case histories are particularly
appropriate there. Occasionally, also, a case history
may be useful a few years after the event, when conditions have so changed for the company involved that
students may discover that "conventional wisdom" both
of company personnel and case writer is subject to re-
appraisal. And in a few instances, case histories contain buried within them the seeds for a new problem
statement and new decision points. In this event, they
can be treated and taught in much the same manner as
problem cases, albeit usually a bit overlong for ease of
use.

However, case histories are useful for transferring
successful managerial experience from one context to
another, in particular if they are discussed by experienced managers who are keen to learn how similar problems were approached and solved in other countries. For
example, the construction management programmes organised
by the ILO Management Development Programme in the
African region include the writing and workshop discussions of case histories on topics such as successful and
unsuccessful ways of organising construction projects,
the establishment and operation of organisations supporting small contractors, or the use of subcontracting for
involving small contractors in larger projects.

Notes to accompany cases

At least two types of writing other than cases have
grown up to accompany case method teaching. These are
"industry notes" and "technical notes". Each has a special form and purpose.

Industry notes are short descriptions of industrial
processes, products, markets and financial information
that focus on a single industry, such as rail transportation, steel-making, the mechanical writing instrument
industry, etc. Such notes are usually to be used as an
additional assignment in conjunction with a cluster of
cases dealing with the same industry. For example,
cases about Coca-Cola Company, Seven-Up Bottling Company,
Dr. Pepper and Royal Crown might be accompanied by a note
on the soft drink industry. Each of the problem cases
can be kept shorter through use of the note. Descriptions of production processes, general materials about
the markets for soft drinks and tables giving published
financial data about all major companies in the industry
can be included in the note and left out of the individual cases.

Such industry notes contain a great deal of knowledge that is useful to students in its own right. Usually the note is written entirely from published sources, without any attempt to do original research into the industry involved. Usually, also, it is not useful to assign a separate class period for the discussion of such a note. But if you have a series of cases dealing with a single industry, you will find a good industry note worth while.

In developed countries, where every university library contains a wealth of books on nearly every subject, and encyclopaedias give write-ups on every modern industry, the industry note is merely a way of saving students time in looking up reference materials. The teacher always has an option of asking students to do the reference work for themselves in the library. In developing countries a good industry note may be the only feasible way for the students to learn about the special aspects of an industry as it applies in their own country. Furthermore, much more of the material in the note will have to be developed from unpublished sources, when you are working in a developing country.

Technical notes are quite different in design and purpose from industry notes. A technical note introduces some concept or technique of analysis. You might want to use a technical note on "break-even analysis", for example, along with a case dealing with a new small business. Or a note on "linear programming by the transportation method" might accompany a case involving deciding which storage depots should be served by various factories.

Technical notes are the case method teacher's response to the often-asked questions "do you force the students to re-invent the wheel?". You don't. You present established techniques, however, in as brief a form as is possible to make them usable by your students, either as notes or in lecturettes.

One alternative to technical notes is to refer students to readings or articles about the techniques involved. When you have access to an article that says just what you want to say about a method, use it. On the other hand, frequently you find that no one article says succinctly everything you want your students to know about a subject, whereas every available article introduces some extraneous material along with its message. It is this situation which may lead you to write a technical note that exactly fits your purpose. You may find that a note of three or four pages, pointed exactly at the need of your students at a particular point in the course, will serve very nicely, even though

it might take 30 pages to do "theoretical justice" to
the technique. Technical notes achieve their brevity
by leaving out the history of thought about the problems,
the proofs and derivations so dear to the heart of
mathematicians and the wealth of examples that are needed
in a "stand-alone" article. You will expect the students to use the note in conjunction with specific cases
introduced at about the same time. You will guide them
in the niceties of the method involved, if they are relevant, and so on. Many articles are written to impress
professional colleagues and not to inform students.
Most textbooks contain far too much detail of examples
and counter-examples to be useful in conjunction with
case method. Specially tailored technical notes are the
result of the need to introduce concepts in case method.

Other topics about cases
and notes

Series cases often result from a long-standing co-
operation between a case writer and a single firm. As
the name suggests, these are a number of cases concerning
the same firm. They may be several cases dealing with
different decision points in the same firm, all described at about the same point in time. Such cases are
particularly useful in policy and strategy courses, where
it is important for students to gain an over-all view of
an organisation, or several organisations, while yet not
having to deal with 150 pages at one sitting. By playing the role of a different manager each day for several
days, and then coming to a case that is set in the
general manager's office, students can gain an understanding of the breadth of the general manager's responsibility.

Another type of series case is a set of cases which
look at the same organisation and the same decision site
over a period of time. Thus you might describe the
situation facing American Motors in 1955, and follow it
with a case in 1961, another in 1968, and so on. Such
a case series partially avoids one of the persistent
criticisms of case method, that it is "static". At the
end of each case in such a series, students would make
their best judgements about what the responsible manager
should do. The next case in the series would pick up
with a description of what the manager actually did, and
how it worked out, before positioning the student to make
the next decision in the series. Incidentally, many
"case histories" might be amenable to being rewritten as
series cases, given the time and interest on the part of
the original case writer. Alternatively, a series of
cases about the same firm can later be converted into a
case history, if so desired.

Clusters of cases dealing with organisations in the same sector have been discussed briefly before, as a justification for an industry note. The strategy of using such clusters of cases deserves mention, however. A cluster of cases in the same industry saves students time in getting familiar with the environment for each new case separately. It allows students to go much more deeply into environmental analysis than cases dealing with different industries each day. Therefore, such case clusters are to be desired, especially for business policy and public management programmes, whenever the teaching site allows for it. It is highly desirable to have a cluster of cases from the textile industry in India, for example, where there is a highly developed and intensely competitive textile industry. Exposing students to knowledge about the textile industry as a setting for learning how to make decisions in a more general sense is good teaching strategy. By contrast, a cluster of cases dealing with the electronics industries of the United States would make very little sense in a developing African nation, where a competitive electronics industry might be a generation away.

This is perhaps just another way of saying that cases for use in particular regions should deal with organisations that are already in the region or are likely to be established in the region in the foreseeable future. Case method is pragmatic. It prepares students to become tomorrow's managers, not tomorrow's theoreticians. It helps managers to enhance their skills, but it does not train them for a future that may be too far ahead.

CASE WRITING

INTRODUCTION TO PART III

Management teachers and trainers in the United States and Europe owe a great debt to several generations of case writers.   There are tens of thousands of cases for teaching management and administration, and a large number of these are in print and available for use at modest cost, in comparison to the substantial cost of writing new cases.   There are far fewer cases set in other regions of the world, and cases specifically appropriate for use in developing countries are especially scarce.   A new generation of case writers must grow up and do the field research to provide the many needed teaching cases set in the developing world.

Even if there were an ample supply of cases available there would be good reason for management teachers to develop skill in case writing.   They need continual exposure to managers who work in the field, in order to remain relevant in teaching.   Just as the doctor-teacher continues to learn more and more about disease by supervising students as they dissect cadavers and treat patients in the teaching hospital, the teacher of management continues to learn by directing students through new field cases.   Many of tomorrow's problems in management have been identified by capturing situations on paper and "dissecting" them at leisure.   Management teachers who get all their own experience from books and theories are likely to have little success in their work.

Case writing, like case teaching and case learning, must finally be learned by doing it.   Some "conventions" of case writing have grown up, however.   Furthermore, early case writers have identified some useful generalisations that will make a new case writer's task easier. The following chapters identify some of these ideas.

CASES BASED ON FIELD RESEARCH 10

Most problem-oriented cases are based on field research. By field research is meant that the case writer visits an organisation whose officials co-operate by giving information. The case writer gathers data, sifts and sorts the material, and finally writes a "case" The responsible executive of the co-operating organisation then agrees in writing to allow the case to be used for teaching purposes. The reasons for each of the above steps and how to carry them out constitute the subject of this chapter.

Finding a case in the field

Several previous references in this book have been made to the need for a case to "fit" into some logical empty space in a course. Perhaps enough attention has been paid to the idea that a case, once written, will serve a teaching purpose. What is not immediately obvious, until you have undertaken a field trip for case writing purposes, is that it is not always easy to "find" a case that fits your purposes. This is especially true of the last few empty spaces in your course. After all, the reason the empty spaces are there is that you have not found any previously written cases that serve your purposes. Just as the empty spaces in the albums of advanced stamp collectors are likely to be those representing the rarest stamps, so too with missing cases for a management course.

But let us begin with an easier starting point. When you start out to write your first case, your purpose is to learn how to find any case and write it. Turning again to another analogy, the beginning butterfly collector seldom catches his rarest butterfly first, but is satisfied to go where there are butterflies and capture any butterfly in good condition.

One of the first things you discover in finding cases in the field is that you can rarely get much information on situations that your co-operating manager is unwilling to talk about. It follows that finding some responsible manager to talk to is a first step in any case writing effort.

The approach. Among the best managers to contact as case sources are those who have been exposed to case method programmes. This may sound almost like a "chicken and egg" proposition in countries that do not have case method teaching programmes. Even in developing countries, however, some industrial leaders can be found who have been educated at business schools where cases are extensively used in teaching or have attended a short case method course somewhere outside their own country. If you are just beginnning, and lack acquaintance with local managers, undertake to give a talk to a business-oriented organisation such as the Rotary Club, Kiwanis or Lions. Let the managers know that you would like to write cases about situations in their firms, and hope one will invite you in to talk.

Sometimes one of your alumni will co-operate with you. If the former student cannot actually release the case, perhaps he/she can introduce you to a higher-level person who can do so. Somehow, you must be allowed to talk to a manager who feels powerful enough and confident enough of the relationship with you, to talk freely and later to release the case.

After case writing efforts have been going on in a country for some time, another way for the beginning case writer to get introductions to co-operative managers is through a colleague who has written a case at a particular site. In fact, when case writing efforts are truly widespread it becomes necessary to keep a central file of the case contacts of all members of the organisation. More is said about this in later instructions for institutions that sponsor case writing efforts.

One approach to case writing about operations and production management is a factory visit. Not all companies are willing to allow outsiders to visit their factories. If you and your class can arrange to visit a factory while it is in operation, however, the possible case writing opportunities are very great. Just as you look around you, you will find that the concepts you teach about factory operation suggest cases. Perhaps you might assign various students to keep track of different details. One might be on the lookout for items under the general heading of "safety". Another might be assigned the job of describing the production process. Another might watch for worker inter-actions and another keep track of "man-machine" ratios and inter-actions. Usually a single factory visit can be the beginning point for several cases. Clearly, however, such cases are not available for writing until you have discussed them with the responsible managers. If your class has experienced the factory visit with you, however, whatever they have seen can become the focal point of vigorous discussion in following classes. Factory visits are in the nature of living cases. The experience of discovering a case situation in the field is an exciting one for most students.

Some approaches to avoid. Several approaches to cases seem very attractive at first glance, yet do not work well. It usually is not a good idea for you to write your first case about a situation in which you yourself are either responsible for action or the victim of some action by your boss. Besides the very real difficulty that arises surrounding release of such a case for teaching purposes, it is impossible for you to write a case about yourself without bias. Another case writer can perhaps write your story without bias, but you yourself cannot.

Another frequent source of cases that never seem to be released is the dissident employee, who tells you about the great wrongs done to him/her by a firm. Once again, there is the problem of bias, as well as the problem of difficulty in getting such a case released.

A third approach that often misfires is to write about a situation you have heard about second-hand, through various informants and the rumour mill. Although you might have enough information in such an instance to avoid bias, you can rarely find anyone who will release the case for teaching, after it is written.

Let us assume, however, that despite difficulties you have contacted a manager who is willing to talk to you about his/her organisation. Let us assume, also, that either he/she has had prior experience with cases or that you have been convincing in describing case method. What comes next will determine whether or not you have a successful case writing experience.

Discuss the manager's needs, not your needs. Most managers, if they are willing to talk business at all, are more willing to discuss the situations they are facing at the moment than they are to speculate on whether or not they have recently "been involved in a capital-budgeting decision". You should try to keep your conversation on business, rather than on football or other matters that do not serve your purpose. But when business is the topic you should listen and try to discover the parallels between what the manager says and what you need. Both your time and that of the manager are expensive, and not to be wasted in trivia, beyond the opening exchanges called for by your culture.

The reason you should listen, rather than describe what you need in a case, is this.   Few managers are expert in abstract thinking.   You, as a case method teacher, make your living by being familiar with both the process of abstraction and the many different ways in which facts can be organised.   For example, the manager may be saying to you, "we are thinking about whether we should change our procedure for shipping between our local factories and our foreign branches.   Perhaps we should consolidate the shipments in a warehouse before sending them out."   He/she may be thinking of this as a change in procedure, as of course it is.   You, on the other hand, should recognise that such a decision involves changes in organisational relationships (which adds a human dimension), a shift in the point where inventories are held (which has definite financial implications), and a need for new functions to be performed (which involves organisational design, among other elements).   In other words, you must try to see in what the manager is saying, the kinds of teaching purposes you could put the situation to.   In effect, while the manager is giving you one situation, you may be identifying a number of cases which could be written about that situation.

Often you will find your case in the files of a co-operating organisation.   That is, it may be a decision the manager made some time in the recent past, or some problem previously solved.   This should cause you no difficulty in case writing.   Instead of reporting the entire history of the situation, you merely need to stop the action at an appropriate point for your students to experience the decision situation.   Although the co-operating manager may be a bit surprised that you do not want to include the report of his/her successful analysis and action, it is you who must decide the nature of your students' learning experience.   About the only problem in writing cases about past situations is in recapturing the "flavour" of uncertainty in the manager's mind.   A second problem is the fact that you must be careful not to include facts that could only become known after the cut-off date for your case.

Keeping track of what you see and hear.   On the first visit with a co-operating manager you may find that if you are obviously keeping notes on your conversation it may put the manager off.   Yet you will need to keep track of your findings.   Probably the best way is to keep the first contact short enough so that you can sit down immediately after the discussion and record most of what went on.   A successful case writing experience requires

more than one contact, in any event.   By your second
visit you may be allowed to take notes.   Some researchers
record conversations on a tape recorder, but this often
seems to hamper the free exchange of ideas.   If your case
requires that you have a nearly verbatim transcript of
what went on at a committee meeting, however, some such
device as a tape recorder may be necessary.

It is most important that you keep track of detailed
facts about the situation, rather than making notes
solely about your impressions of the situation.   Although
you must abstract from the details to identify the nature
of the case you are about to write, the case itself must
be made up of details.   If you merely take notes in the
form of abstractions, you will find it difficult later on
to recapture the necessary low-level facts to put in the
case.   It may be useful to give an example or two of
this distinction.

Suppose that you learn, from the manager you are
talking to, that the firm is being squeezed between ris-
ing costs and a government ceiling on prices.   Its costs
are now 87% of their allowed selling price.   Costs are
made up of raw materials (55%), direct labour (30%),
fixed overhead (10%) and general administrative (5%).
If you record these details, you can later on construct
a very useful pro forma operating statement.   If, on the
other hand, you record your impression as "cost-profit
squeeze", you will later be at a loss to recall details
for the case.

As another example, on a factory tour, you may
observe clusters of employees at various points on the
factory floor apart from the machinery.   If you record
the impression, "substantial idleness of labour", you may
miss the fact that one of the groups was clustered about
a foreman, receiving verbal instructions, whereas other
groups were taking advantage of the foreman's preoccupa-
tion to take a break from work.   If you later record in
your case "there was substantial idleness among the
workers", you will not be wrong, but the fact will not be
particularly useful to students studying the case.   The
more detailed observation of what was going on, however,
would open up possibilities for remedial action.

Confidentiality.   Often the point is made by
teachers in developing countries, "we cannot get managers
to talk about their business.   What works in America
cannot be made to work here".   This is often a valid concern.   Certainly it is far easier to find co-operative
managers in a culture where cases have been written and
used for many years.   None the less, experience has
proved that one can persuade managers to co-operate in
nearly every country and region.   Usually the difficulty

arises around some form of fear over loss of confidentiality. Sometimes the manager's concern for confidentiality becomes aroused just at the point where you start to take notes, and particularly when you are taking notes about a damaging fact.

You must convince the manager of two things. The first is short-range confidentiality and the second is long-range disguise. Confidentiality means that the recorded facts will not be disclosed to anyone until you have completed your case and the manager has read it and formally released it for teaching purposes. One of the justifications for the release procedure is to quiet the manager's fears about exposure until you have a chance to record your entire case. Often you will gather far more material than you actually use in the case, and you cannot spend the time convincing the manager that you will keep confidential each new piece of information. Guaranteeing confidentiality of all information until the case is completed saves your and the manager's time.

If you are writing a case for your own course, this guarantee is not difficult for you to make, although you may have some difficulty in persuading the manager of the confidentiality of matters that are processed by a typist and duplicated by someone in a photocopy room. If you are a case writer who works for a teacher the circle of confidants becomes a bit wider. When you are a member of a case writer's workshop the question of what will be shared with colleagues before the case is finished is even a bit more touchy. Usually the burden of convincing the co-operating manager about confidentiality falls on the shoulders of the most prestigious person who will know the facts about the situation before it is disguised. Somehow you must gain the respect of the co-operating manager, or you will get no further with the case.

Not only must the facts of the case be kept confidential until the manager has "signed off" on the case for teaching purposes, but for the long run it may be necessary to "disguise" a case by changing the names of case characters, the name and location of the company, and so on. More will be said about techniques of disguising later in this chapter, but it is worth mentioning here that it usually is virtually impossible to disguise the nature of the company's product, where the case involves either marketing or production processes. If the company is virtually the only manufacturer of sheet steel in the country, for example, and it is necessary to disguise the firm, it may be necessary to locate the company in a "mythical" country, that is a country with an invented name, such as "Ongolia" or "Paradiso".

It cannot be emphasised enough that there is a difference between case writing and investigative reporting or journalism. It only takes a few instances where a case writer has violated the confidences of a co-operative manager for case writing to be set back for years in a country or region. The author has heard of an instance where a case method student, introduced to a co-operating firm by his professor, wrote an "exposé" and submitted it to a newspaper. Even though he "disguised" the name of the firm, the facts of the situation were so easily identified with the company involved that it caused considerable hurt feelings. Not only did the co-operating company discipline the manager who had talked to the student, it was difficult for anyone to do case writing in that country for some time thereafter.

Writing the case

Sometimes after the first visit and discussion with a co-operating manager, and certainly before you have spent more than two visits, you should have a good idea whether or not you can develop a case at that site. Before you spend additional time in gathering information you should set down a short prospectus for the case you plan to write. This will serve to remind you of your intentions. It should also be the basis for a short discussion with the co-operating manager. Unless you have an agreement at this stage that the case can probably be released, it is not a good bet to proceed. A great many good teaching cases languish in case writers' files because they were refused a release after a lot of work was put in on them. In many instances you will need information from other people in the organisation or from company documents. If the co-operating manager has agreed on a case focus, he/she will more readily understand why you need the additional information.

Data gathering. Once past the initial interview stage, data gathering becomes more directive and oriented to your purpose. You must discover what happened to whom, when it happened and where, all basic questions of descriptive research. If your respondents have ideas about why things happened, you will need to keep track of their opinions. If you are writing a case about a decision made in the past, you must understand how the decision was made. If you are studying an ongoing situation, you must discover how the decision maker plans to use facts and concepts to solve the existing problem.

For the purposes of your case, however, you will often need more. For example, you may find that a manager seemed to ignore environmental facts in reaching a decision. If you want your students to learn how to integrate environmental analysis into their decisions, you will need to include such facts in the case you are writing. As another example, the manager may have made a sales forecast somewhat intuitively, without explicit reference to past sales data. Knowing that your students cannot rely on their intuition, you may decide to gather data about past sales to include in your case.

In some even more extreme instance, you may believe that the manager involved did not understand the problem well, and therefore acted on less information than was readily available. Once again, you will want to provide your students with as much of the relevant information as you can gather.

The more you step out of the role of passive fact gatherer and press the co-operating manager for facts you believe should have been considered important, the more risk you run of losing your case. Learning the limits on such extra research is a matter of experience. If you must stretch the situation entirely "out of shape" to match your need for a case, you probably should drop it and look for another co-operating organisation. On the other hand, if you can serve your purpose by adding no more than about 25% of additional information to that originally available, this is probably reasonable.

You should note, however, that the additional information is not "invented". It all should be data that pertain to the actual situation and were available to the decision maker. The strongest reason for writing a case in the field rather than from an armchair is to preserve the natural complexities and inter-relationships of facts. When you invent facts to embellish a field case you cannot be sure of the effect on the students.

There are a good many ways to develop "real-world" facts to add to a case. One example may suggest the ingenuity that is required. A case was being written about a small hotel, owned by a man and his wife who had little experience in the hotel business. They knew their own operating figures, but had not made any attempt to find standards of comparison so that they could tell whether they were doing well or not. The case writer knew that published data were available giving typical operating statistics for small hotels. By including an exhibit showing such typical operating data, the case writer was able to provide an effective standard of comparison. The important point was that such a standard was available to the managers, although they had not used it.

Conventions of case writing. As pointed out in Chapter 1, several useful conventions have grown up in

writing cases.   Probably the most important of these
concerns they way in which data are presented.   Anything
you consider to be a "true fact", beyond challenge by the
student, you should state as a declaratory sentence.   In
effect you as the case writer are putting your guarantee
of authenticity on all such facts.   You are saying, "if
you had been there, you would have discovered these
facts".

You may wish to qualify facts slightly, as might be
the case regarding observations you make on a factory
visit.   "A visitor to the factory at 3 p.m. on Wednesday
afternoon observed several groups of workers engaged in
active discussions, away from their machines."   Students
realise that the presence of strange visitors in a factory can have an effect on worker behaviour.   This method
of reporting allows the students to decide, based on other
evidence as well, whether what was observed was "typical"
behaviour.

A third important category of case facts is the
opinions held by case characters.   Perhaps the co-
operating manager has told you, "the problem is one of
low worker morale".   It is important for you to preserve
this as an opinion as you write your case.   If you
declare low worker morale to be a problem, you give the
students no way to challenge the opinion.

Another convention of case writing is to write cases
in the past tense.   Although it may seem a bit artificial,
at first, to describe an ongoing company and its present
situation in the past tense, it is worth while to do so.
Cases written in the past tense can be used again and
again in future years and in other environments without
losing their appeal.

The body of the case then starts far enough back in
history to allow you to present the details of case data
in a comfortable order.   If the case is a long one, this
section may be divided into topics identified by subheadings (e.g. "Company history", "Products", "Processes",
"Marketing", etc.).   Cases of less than four pages
rarely need subheadings.   As you describe the situation
you should introduce facts in chronological order, where
feasible.   By doing this you will arrive at the end of
the body of the case at the date specified in the opening.
Your closing paragraphs can then establish what you expect
the students to do.   The body of the case thus represents an extensive "flashback" between the opening and
closing.

It is essential for the body of the case to be written in effective prose style.   There is a temptation,
particularly in cases where some mathematical technique

is involved, to lapse into mathematical notation and other condensed ways of presenting data. You should resist this temptation. Facts in the real world do not often appear in condensed form. One of the skills you are trying to teach is the process of condensing. An exception to this is the case whose purpose is to teach students how to use and interpret the condensed notations themselves.

A final useful convention, which is sometimes successfully violated, is to exclude the case writer as a case character. Often the inclusion of the case writer is a distraction that serves no useful purpose in class discussion. One major exception to this convention is in certain human relations cases, where it is clearly the presence of the case writer, a neutral outsider, that moves case characters to talk about their feelings. Such cases are more believable because the case writer appears than they would be otherwise. As a general rule, the author recommends that you leave yourself out of the case if you can see how to do so.

Another design feature of cases, which lies somewhere between a convention and precept, is that you avoid inserting your conclusions in the case. It cannot be emphasised enough that the purpose of a teaching case is to give students the experience of analysing and judging situations. A fundamental aspect of analysis is the discovery of hidden cause-effect relationships. If you plainly state a cause-effect relationship, you must realise that you have taken out of the students' hands the whole line of reasoning that led up to the discovery of the relationship. The same precept is true of your biases regarding "right" and "wrong" solutions to case problems. Students must learn how to develop judgement and they can best do it as they study an unbiased case.

The best way to avoid unconscious attributions of cause-effect relationships and/or bias is to stay at a very low level of abstraction in writing a case. Report "what, when, where and to whom", and leave out "why and how", except as the last two items reflect opinions of case characters.

It is well to admit that the case writer has an impact on the students' learning experience by choosing to include some facts in the case and to exclude others. This is an irreducible minimum of the intrusion of your opinions, about which more is said a little later.

A useful format for a case is shown as figure 6. You will find a good many cases that do not follow this format, but it provides a useful checklist for the beginning case writer.

Figure 6   A general case format

Opening: (First few paragraphs)	Name and title of responsible manager Name, location and product line of organization Date Synopsis of decision or problem setting

Case body:	Company history, if relevant
	Environmental facts, if relevant
	Expanded description of the decision or problem situation
	    Organizational relationships
	    Other case characters
	    Products and processes
	    Financial data
	    Marketing information
	    Human interaction facts
	    etc.

Closing: (Last paragraph or two)	Scenario to establish a sense of urgency about the problem or decision

The key to the format is the opening section, which often is as short as a single paragraph. In simple prose it should set the scene for the students. By quickly introducing the responsible manager by name and title, it tells the students what role they are to play. By giving a specific date (month and year, typically), it establishes an environmental context. By identifying the company it quickly tells the students whether they have much or little previous experience that will be relevant in the analysis. Finally, by stating the decision or problem setting, at least as seen by the manager, it helps students prepare for their analysis of what is to follow.

Cases often contain certain conventional condensations, as well. After students have learned how to construct balance sheets and operating statements, for example, cases can effectively show financial data in the form of these conventional reports. Sometimes you may want to include exhibits such as charts, graphs and tables, along with prose, to present large amounts of quantitative data succinctly. Your teaching purpose for the case will determine how much or how little organising of the data you do beforehand, and how much you leave for students to do.

The same can be said about the decision to include or exclude information. In nearly every instance you will have gathered far more information than is feasible to include in your case. What you should seek is a compromise between the "stripped-down" case that gives only the minimum information needed to use a single analytical technique and a case that includes "everything". The former is primarily an "example" of an application of a technique, while the latter would be a "slice of life", with few if any clues to the student about how to proceed. Most cases fall somewhere between these extremes. You should include all the data you explicitly expect students to use, plus some other facts you believe are also relevant. In some instances case writers include completely irrelevant or even confusing data as a challenge to students. Unfortunately, such cases often also confuse other teachers and, as a result, they are not much used except by their authors.

One way to ensure that you are including relevant data is to write a concurrent analysis of the case, alongside your writing of the case itself. When you discover that your analysis requires information you have not included in the case, you can put it in. Sometimes your analysis calls for data you have not even gathered. In such instances you should return to the field to get the missing data. Your concurrent analysis is the place for you to insert your own ideas of cause and effect and your own biases. These abstractions will be useful to you in writing a teaching note. Your concurrent analysis will also help to identify facts you have included in the case but which may be "extra", at least in the sense that you have not needed them for your own analysis. There is no rule about how much extra information is "too much". If you find, however, that the case you are writing will reach or exceed the upper limit on length for practical use in your culture, it is best to remove some of the extra information.

Cut-off point. Each case should have a definite cut-off point. Logically, this is the date or time when the problem arises or the decision must be made. Of course you do not want to include information in the case that occurred after the cut-off point. This is mainly a problem with cases about past decisions (cases written "from the files"). It also sometimes arises when you gather data over an extended period about a currently active situation. One way to avoid including post-dated material is to date your notes and to pay particular attention to the applicable dates of memoranda in the files.

A sense of urgency is often interjected in the last paragraph of a case. This is one of the few places where some invention enters into field cases. Often it is difficult to identify exactly the state of mind of the co-operating manager at the time of the cut-off point. In order to recreate the sense of urgency, therefore, the

last paragraph may set a special imaginary scene.   For
example, in a case where the manager is considering taking disciplinary action with a subordinate, the last
paragraph may say, "just as Peter Smith had finished reviewing the facts of the situation in his mind he saw
Tom Jones, his subordinate, approaching his office.   He
wondered what action he should take."

The important element to keep in mind about the
sense of urgency is that it should appear to allow time
for the sort of thinking the student must do about the
case.   An elaborate five-year plan would not be worked
out while the manager was on his way between his office
and the board room for a meeting.   In such a case the
urgency might be suggested by, "John Castle realised that
he must be prepared, three weeks hence, to present his
plans to the regular meeting of the board of directors".

Questions are sometimes printed at the end of cases
to direct students' attention to various types of analysis.   Although these may be relatively useful in printed
case books, the author prefers not to see them on loose-
leaf cases.   The presence of a particular set of questions makes it difficult for a teacher to use the case in
a different way.   Questions may also suggest viewpoints
that some teachers would prefer to have their students
develop on their own.   If you believe some questions
would assist others in using the case, put them in the
teaching note.   Let other teachers select the questions
that fit their own purposes.

Disguise.   A case may need to be disguised before
the co-operating manager will release it for use.   The
most frequent form of disguise is to change all names in
the case, including the name of the organisation.
Usually this is accompanied by a change in the city of
location.   A deeper disguise involves changing the
quantitative facts of the case.   Only rarely is it possible to disguise the industry, except in cases where the
focus is almost entirely on human relations, where industry may be unimportant to the teaching purpose.   Each
part of the process of disguising the case is worth a
short word of explanation.

The first step is to write the case in plain language, undisguised, and check it with the co-operating
manager for accuracy.   It is very difficult to write the
case first in disguised form, and it is even harder for
the manager to be sure you have kept the character list
straight when all there is to work with is the disguised
names.   Only after writing a satisfactory undisguised
case should you start the disguise process.

The choice of a new company name involves two problems. The new name should be enough different from the actual one to be a good disguise. For example, you would not want to substitue "Giant Electric" for "Gigantic Electric". The other problem is to avoid substituting a name which is in use by an existing company in the same or a related industry. In industrialised countries it is a little difficult to think of a name that is not in use somewhere, but there are good directories of companies in which to check on the matter. In developing countries the choice of a new name is not as difficult, but directories are less available and complete.

Some case writers try to avoid this difficulty by calling their company the "ABC Company", or "XYZ, Inc.". There is nothing ethically wrong with this approach, but it is not good teaching strategy. Students find it difficult to get deeply interested in obviously fictitious companies. The same is true of fictitious products, identified only as "product X" or "widgets".

The selection of a new company location is again less of a problem in developed countries, where many cities are sufficiently large and diversified to serve the purpose. In such situations, it is only necessary to be sure that size and distance relationships that are important to the situation are preserved. Cases involving transportation and distribution are sometimes a little tricky to disguise by changing locations, even in the United States. In developing areas of the world the problem of location disguise is more difficult to solve, since in many countries there is only one industrial city. In such situations it may be best to fictionalise the city and country involved, since such cases usually also involve a unique industrial unit.

The invention of a new cast of characters is not much of a problem in most industrialised countries, but is more of a problem, the author believes, in places like India and Africa. In America or in Europe you have a large selection of names that are not obviously identified with race, ethnic origin, caste or tribe. So long as the case problem is not itself one that arises from racial or ethnic differences, one list of case character names is much like another. The process of changing names is merely one of building a list of original names, choosing an equal number of different names and carefully making the changes in the case. One wants to avoid choosing names that are so much alike that they may be confused, such as "Mr. Jones, Mr. Johns and Mr. Jonas" but apart from that the process has few pitfalls.

In cultures where tribe or caste is important, however, the case writer must take care in renaming the

characters, because names reveal tribe and/or caste. If
a company has been disguised by moving it from Ahmedabad
to Calcutta, India, for example, its executives and
workers must have names appropriate to the new region and
the relative status among the various positions and the
names of people who hold them must be preserved.
Although there are no doubt situations where the differences in status should not influence decisions, still
such differences are there in the situation, and should
be retained for the student to evaluate. It goes without saying that each case writer is more familiar with
name-status relationships in his/her own culture. Only
when you are writing cases in a culture different from
your own are you likely to have extreme difficulty with
this part of the disguise process.

Numbers should be disguised in such a way as to preserve the ratios among them. Ratios are the substance
of most analytical techniques involving quantity. For
example, all total sales, costs and investment figures
can be multiplied by a single multiplier, such as 1.31
(which results in larger disguised figures) or 0.73
(which results in smaller figures). If the unit price
of a product is well known, as for many years was true of
chewing gum in the United States, the total unit volume
should be adjusted by multiplying it by the same constant.
If the unit price can vary, you have a choice of adjust-
ing either the price or the physical volume of units.
Of course, if any of the quantities in the original case
are reported in ratio form (price-earnings ratio, for
example) you do not multiply the ratio by the constant.

Even after having changed the numbers by the constant multiplier, you should redo all your concurrent
analysis calculations. This will help you check that
the important relationships have not been disturbed. It
will also help you to prepare your teaching note, which
must be consistent with the disguised case in every
detail.

Release. It is then the final product, the disguised case, which you present to the co-operating
manager for review and release. When you have a signed
release, you are ready to try the case in class, to see
if students react as you hoped they would. Often a
field case will need some rewriting after this class
trial. Rewritten cases are then resubmitted for release,
and taught again. Only when you are satisfied that the
case "works well" for its intended purpose are you ready
to let it out of your own hands for use by others,
through a clearing-house or library.

The release should be obtained in something like the
form below:

I have read the case, (case name) prepared by
(author's name), and I hereby authorise the case to be
used for teaching purposes, including reproduction in
case books or as loose-leaf cases.

Date: _____   Signed: _____

                            Title: _____

                            Organisation: _____

The original signed release should be kept in the
author's case file or in a file established to this
effect by the author's institution. Although it is
highly unlikely that a properly prepared and released
case will create controversy later on, the release is the
case writer's protection against accusations of impropriety.

OTHER CASES AND NOTES

11

Although the bulk of all cases in print are based on field research, other sources of information for cases are sometimes used. As indicated in an earlier chapter, at times there may be current issues that influence decision makers, about which you want your students to think deeply. Yet it is just these issues about which managers are least willing to allow cases to be written. Environmental pollution, discriminatory practices in hiring and ethical issues including bribery are examples of topics about which, at times, it has been difficult to get co-operative managers to give information. Another class of topics about which it is sometimes difficult to get detailed field cases is those decisions for which a new technique has been recently developed. You will certainly want your students to be prepared to use the new technique when they reach managerial stature, yet few business firms may yet be using the technique, or organising their data in ways necessary for use of the technique. These circumstances and others have led case writers to develop cases based on published documents (or "library" cases) and cases based on "generalised experience", by which is meant that the cases are largely made up in the mind of the case writer.

In addition to cases based on other than field research, three useful types of notes must be written from time to time. These are the industry note, the technical note and teaching notes. Later paragraphs of this chapter suggest ways of preparing these notes.

Cases based on published documents

A case based on published documents often appears very much like a field research case, in that it can be cast as a description of a situation, written in the past tense, and intersperses prose with exhibits and graphs. Occasionally the case writer is skilful enough to

introduce a named manager who is faced with a problem.
Depending upon the type of published documents used, it
is often possible to use an effective set of quotations
of case characters. For example, if one source of
material is a series of annual reports of a company, it
is possible to develop quotations from the president's
letter to stockholders portion of the reports. These do
not deal with minor matters, of course, but can give some
indication of the public face that management has put
upon the happenings of each past year, at least.

Newspaper accounts of newsworthy events, such as
strikes, lawsuits and natural disasters, often contain a
great deal of information gathered by journalists.
Court documents themselves are sometimes useful as
sources of information and quotations. Government
agency reports are in the public domain. Public agencies publish reports of investigations; such reports
are often full of useful information. Public relations
handouts of companies tell a great deal about what those
companies want the public to know about controversial
issues. It would seem almost easy to write a case about
any issue that had resulted in a public hearing.

. In such instances, the difficulty does not arise
because of too little data. There is usually far too
much to use, and even sometimes far too much to dig
through in trying to find what you want to use for your
case. Furthermore, there is the problem that every
statement in published documents is tailored to fit the
particular audience for that document. Publicity releases of companies are meant to convince the public of
the viewpoint that the company finds useful. Quotations
from labour leaders about companies against which their
unions are presently on strike are sure to be negative.

Even quotations drawn from testimony in court cases
or government hearings are difficult to interpret.
Although you may be fairly certain that answers to direct
questions under oath are "true", you may not always find
them very informative, since they are often narrowly
responsive to pointed questions. In short, every printed document you must look at to discover material for
your case is written from a different point of view and
directed at a different audience. Thus it will often be
difficult for you to find information of the unbiased
sort that usually makes for the best cases. Unfortunately, a collection of data from different biases does
not add up to one unbiased viewpoint.

Occasionally, recognising the fact that such biases
cannot be avoided, a "case" is put together which consists entirely of copies of various documents, each
carefully identified with its viewpoint. Although this

brings biases into the open, it often results in a fairly
dull case for students to discuss, since there is almost
no way for them to discover the important low-level facts
on which to base their personal searches for cause and
effect and judgements about right and wrong.   What it
finally comes down to is that relatively few cases based
on published information become excellent teaching
vehicles, although they often are about all one can find
concerning certain important issues of the day.

Sometimes it is possible to get an organisation to
co-operate in letting you write a case about them when it
becomes clear that you can write a nearly complete case
based on published documents.   It is courteous for you
to send a copy of the case to a responsible executive of
the company, in any event.   If this results in an offer
to give you access to internal data you may wish to
accept the chance to turn the case into a field case.
Remember, however, that a field case will require release
in its entirety before you can use it, whereas a case
written entirely from published sources does not require
release.   If you use extensive direct quotations from
the published sources, of course, the usual requirements
for permission to quote must be obtained from copyright
holders.

One other form of case drawn from published sources
(and sometimes from old files of the organisation, as
well) is so specialised that it is only mentioned here.
That is the business history case.   Some such cases run
to multiple published volumes, and require an understanding of historical documentation and other research techniques that are far beyond the scope of this manual.

Cases based on "generalised experience"

Some case writers have such a breadth of experience
through long years of case writing and consulting with
organisations throughout the world, that they can write
cases based on "generalised experience" without fear of
anyone's challenging the worth of the cases.   As was
stated in an earlier chapter, some "classic" cases have
such a source.   Most case writers, lacking such long
experience, turn to writing "armchair" cases either
because they desperately need a case for which they have
been unable to find a real-world field source or because
they are too lazy to do the field research.   Neither of
these excuses is usually a very good one.   If you cannot
find a real-world source for a case, there should be at
least a suspicion in your mind that the topic is not one
best covered by a case.   If you do not enjoy case writing so much that it is more pleasant to gather field
cases than to write armchair cases, then perhaps you are
better off writing lectures!

After such a negative statement, however, let us admit that there are times when every case method teacher faces the need to write a short case to fit a niche in his/her course. Even though the case when it is finished will be more like an extended "example" than a true field case, it may still be more effective in teaching students how to use some new technique than a lecture. How do you go about writing such a case?

The closer the case can come to an actual field situation, the better. Although the decision structure you want to teach to the students will determine the nature of the information you will need to include, the "trappings" of the data can come from your experience. Perhaps you have had a chance to visit several iron foundries. You could easily cite a case describing methods improvement in a foundry. Your case would then contain a description of the foundry process, a somewhat composite picture of the foundry workplace, containing common elements from all the foundries you have visited. You may not have seen the particular decision or problem setting at any one of the foundries. In fact, if you had seen such a setting, you would be back seeking a field case. But you may be able to imagine the situation arising in your composite foundry. Your experience with foundries will also tell you what some of the effective ratios and relationships are - number of workers per furnace and per square foot of factory, pay-roll costs as a percent of sales, size of typical work gangs, and the like. If these items are needed to give realism to your case, the more experience you have with the industry the more realistic your case will be.

The author believes that there is one main temptation surrounding "generalised experience" cases, which is to attribute a field research case to "generalised experience" because the field case failed to be released. Each case writer will have to search his/her own conscience before falling to such a temptation. There is little doubt but that a well-disguised case will protect the writer from open hostility by the co-operating manager. But if a great many cases were published in this way, the climate for writing field cases might become far less hospitable. As may be inferred from the above statements, the "release for teaching purposes" of a generalised experience case is signed by the case writer.

Industry notes

The structure of industry notes has been described in Chapter 9. It remains only to give some suggestions about how to write them. Such notes are intended to make clearer to students the nature of industries, and the important relationships among inputs, production processes, outputs and markets, including the competitive environment. Usually such notes support a cluster of cases dealing with the industry, but occasionally they will be written to accompany a case that would otherwise be too long if the important material in the note were included in the case. An industry note drawn from published source materials does not require release.

One of the first places to start in describing production processes is the encyclopaedia. Often it gives an excellent non-technical account of how some product (e.g. cement) is made. It will often tell you whether there are two or more competitive production processes (in the case of cement, for example, wet and dry processes) and the relative merits of each. Sometimes an industry association puts out public relations material that gives a good description of processes, and diagrams that aid in understanding the processes. It goes without saying that if you quote substantially from such sources, and particularly if you copy a diagram, that you should request permission to use the quoted material and give credit to the source.

Other information that often appears in industry notes regards the economics of the industry in the relevant country or area. In the United States the Census of Manufactures gives such information as numbers of production units by annual capacity, annual sales and a host of other information that may fit your purpose in writing the note. It is often useful to indicate the share of the market held by the top few companies; this information, too, is often publicly available.

Industry notes for developing countries are far less likely to be written solely from published sources. Often you must depend upon the co-operation of the company that is giving you the case. If the technology of a particular factory is somewhat older than that reported in current encyclopaedias, you may have to draw carefully upon observation and the descriptions given you by the factory manager. Sometimes you may find such older technology described in earlier editions of encyclopaedias, or in engineering textbooks of prior years. As for market size and the competitive environment, you may have to depend upon the expert knowledge of individuals engaged in the industry, if government statistics are unavailable in such detail.

Whether you get the material for industry notes from published sources or from interviews, however, it is well to remember that it is your purpose to make the information easily available to your students. Thus you should practice simplifying the matter, rather than

giving every detail that might be reported.   If a word
in the reference was unfamiliar to you until you had
looked it up, do not use the word in the note unless you
give a definition the first time it appears.   For
example, in a note about the paper industry the word
"furnish", as a short-hand way of referring to any one of
a number of raw materials that could be used to make
paper, is such a useful word that you might well want to
use it throughout the note, after being careful to define
it the first time it was used.

Technical notes

The technical note serves yet a different purpose,
to introduce students to analytical concepts and decision-
making models.   Such notes vary from a paragraph or two
of extended definition of a jargon word or phrase to
several pages of explanation of a theory and examples of
the theory's application.   Once again, the reason for
such notes is to make available in its simplest form the
idea you want your students to grasp.   Very frequently
you will base such notes on several textbook descriptions
of the idea you are developing.   Rarely will what you
are writing be the result of original research on your
part.

Usually you write such notes when you are not satisfied with the way other authors have put the matter.
Presumably, if you found another author who said things
just as you liked, you could arrange to get reprint
rights for that part of the author's work that was useful
to you.   But many authors, even of textbooks, are inc-
lined to describe analytical techniques as if they were
things of beauty in themselves, rather than useful tools
for use in making practical decisions.   Almost always
you can write what is needed in fewer words than used by
the originators of the ideas.   And, by leaving out such
of the finer subtleties of the models as have little use
in practice, you can make the techniques far clearer to
your students than do the basic works from which you
distil your note.   Once again, long quotations should
generally be avoided, and any such quotations and use of
other authors' exhibits should be acknowledged and permission obtained for using them.   The usual rules of
copyright apply.   Beyond this, a technical note does not
require a release for use in teaching.

Teaching notes

As has been clearly suggested in earlier chapters,
each teacher eventually decides how to use a case, based
on his/her own preferences.   Given this fact, even the
abstracts of cases that are written by case writers do
not determine fully how a case will be used by someone

else. None the less, it has been the experience of most case book publishers, and also of clearing-house operators, that cases that are accompanied by teaching notes written by the authors are far more in demand than otherwise.

A teaching note is a separate document, which is identified with its appropriate case by a single different digit in the identification number. It is restricted in its distribution, being made available by clearing-houses or publishers only to bona fide teachers or trainers. Its purpose is to assist the teacher or trainer in using the accompanying case. It may take several forms and have a fairly wide range of content.

Usually the teaching note gives some information about the case writer's purpose in writing the case. If the case is disguised, the teaching note does not break the disguise. However, sometimes the case writer includes in the teaching note some events that occurred after the cut-off point of the case. It may tell the actions taken by the manager and their outcomes. Occasionally the teaching note gives additional information about the case situation, in order to allow the teacher to answer common questions that arise from students. When the case writer has had considerable experience with the case, the teaching note often tells something about the reactions of various types of students to the case.

When the case contains a great deal of quantitative data, the teaching note frequently offers several ways of utilising the data. At the very least it suggests techniques the author has found useful in analysing the information. More elaborate teaching notes give the detail of the various analytical techniques and the answers that arise from using the techniques. Lists of questions the case writer believes are useful in guiding students through the case may be included in the teaching note.

There is, of course, the risk that the case writer may imply that there is only one right way to use a case. This would imply, as well, that there was only one right solution to the case problem. If you believe you are giving this impression with your teaching note, you have probably gone too far in including detail in it. If you can think of yourself sitting down with a colleague and discussing your experiences with the case in a way that would be helpful to anyone using it, your teaching note will probably be effective.

PART IV

CASE METHOD TEACHING SYSTEM COMPONENTS

INTRODUCTION TO PART IV

Up to this point we have discussed cases, case
teaching, and case writing in a context of students who
learn and teachers who teach.   For case method truly to
have an impact on the management habits of a country,
however, several other components of a system must be in
place.   Just as earlier chapters warned students that
case method makes special demands on their time and
attention and told teachers that case method requires
extra preparation on their part, this section covers
points of interest to institutions that become committed
to case method.

An individual professor or trainer can teach by
cases at an institution that feels no particular commitment to case method.   But if an institution believes
that case method should be fostered, it is necessary to
commit resources to this effort.   Particularly in
developing countries, where teachers cannot easily be in
contact with nearby case method installations, institutions must create special sorts of support systems for
case development, case distribution and case use.

Chapter 12 deals with the many facets of an institution's adapting to the addition of case courses to
their curricula.   Chapter 13 introduces important criteria for designing a case writing workshop, one of the
single most important activities needed to promote case
method teaching in new areas.   Chapter 14 mentions a
number of other considerations involved in institutional
support of case method teaching.   It also treats with
the special needs of developing countries for cases and
case method teaching and refers to some unique problems
in developing cases in such areas.

INTRODUCING CASE METHOD IN A SINGLE INSTITUTION

12

It is not immediately apparent to many heads of institutions that there should be anything special about introducing case method teaching at their institutions. Perhaps many get started in this direction after thinking something like the following: "Our institution should be as up to date as any. What is the harm in sending a couple of our bright young staff members to a case method workshop and letting them teach by this new method when they return?" In fact, however, to introduce case method effectively requires special attention to teaching staff, physical facilities, case selection, duplication and case writing potential, as well as the development of new types of courses and programmes to exploit the full potential of the method.

Teaching staff

As may be clear from preceding chapters, a teacher does not become proficient in using cases overnight. Institutions (like the Indian Institute of Management at Ahmedabad) which have made a complete commitment to case method, have found it useful to send every new faculty member through advanced educational training at universities were case method is heavily used. At the very least each faculty member who is to teach by cases should have had considerable exposure to case method. There are several ways to accomplish this.

One is to seek young teachers who have received their advanced management education in universities where case method is extensively used. Although Harvard Business School is best known as a case method school, several other universities and institutes around the world also introduce their students to large numbers of cases.

A second method is to select young teachers who have an interest in case method teaching and send them for their terminal degrees to one of the same institutions. A third approach, and one that is available to industrial units who wish to train their trainers in case method, is to seek out shorter programmes in which case method is used for the instruction. Such programmes, called "management development programmes" or "advanced management programmes", are offered in many parts of the world. Their principal focus is not upon displaying particular teaching methods, but upon the specific knowledge of skill content of the course. For the accounting teacher who would like to learn how to teach by cases, however, attending a few-week course in accounting, ably conducted by case method, would have the double benefit of letting the teacher brush up on new ideas in the field and become acquainted with case method and a number of specific cases useful in dealing with the relevant concepts.

A final approach is for the institution itself to become involved, alone or with sister institutions, in developing case method programmes, perhaps such as the case writers' workshops which are more fully described in a later chapter. Along with the other encouragement and support actions mentioned later on, these workshops will tend to demonstrate the institution's commitment to case method. The author believes that no teacher is truly a "case method person" until he/she has written cases in the field as well as taught by cases for some time.

Another important element of promoting case method, which follows from the above belief, is that case writing must be rewarded by the institution. More is said about this in Chapter 14. Suffice it to say here that few institutions have yet discovered an appropriate formula for recognising the intellectual effort involved in good case writing. Yet such recognition is critical if teachers are to be willing to spend the time involved in writing field cases.

Physical facilities

Whether extensive physical changes will be needed to promote case method in an institution depends on many things. If class sizes are typically between 20 and 50 students at the institution, case method need not change class size. If the typical classroom is of the right size and shape, no change is required. But it is useful to review the minimum requirements for case method, and then to detail a few of the adjustments that can be made to use the method to its fullest potential.

Class size for case method should be between 15 and
50 students per class.   The author has taught by case
method in groups of 100 or in groups as small as 6, and
it is possible, other conditions being ideal, to retain
many benefits of case method at each extreme.   There are
some very good reasons why classes should be larger than
15 and smaller than 50, however.

For some reason that is not fully understood,
experience has shown that about one-third of the students in a class, almost no matter of what size, will be
well prepared on any given day.   If the class is too
small, therefore, the teacher finds it difficult to
develop lively discussion within and among the student
group.   Thus what usually happens in very small classes
is that the teacher carries on a series of two-way conversations with the students.   This requires a great
deal of ingenuity of the teacher, and gives the students
too little experience in developing group discussions.

At the other extreme of size, that same fact of one-
third of the students being prepared presents the teacher
with another dilemma.   If more than 15 students are to be
heard patiently as they present their ideas, the time in
a regular class period becomes too short.   One result
is often that the teacher feels forced to cut a student's
recitations short, "in order to give others a chance to
recite".   This can encourage students to be satisfied
with shallow or narrow analyses of the cases, since they
expect not to be forced to reveal a broad and deep
appraisal.

If an institution physically gathers students in
very large groups to hear lectures, the change to case
method-sized classes has obvious budgetary implications.
One would need either a larger number of teachers or a
larger number of teaching hours per faculty member.
Each of these has its costs, as experienced administrators know without being told.   Even at an institution
which has some large lecture courses, however, there are
usually many advanced courses with small class sizes.
This suggests that case method should first be introduced
in the advanced classes, which is a good introductory
strategy.

Classroom layout should also be changed.   An efficient lecture hall for a group of 50 students may be a
room with 6 seats across, arranged in 9 rows deep.   Such
a room is deadly for case method teaching.   The students
in the rear can see only the pates of the students in
front of them, and they seldom can hear a recitation
from the front of the room.   The teacher can barely
recognise the individual student in the rear, and hear
poorly what is being said at the back of the classroom.

Case method is best conducted in a room laid out as is shown in figure 7. The room shown provides swivel-action seats for 55 students. Each outer tier of tables and seats is raised a few inches above the one in front to provide better lines of sight between students and the front of the room. The room shown here is a rough representation of a case method classroom first developed at Harvard Business School over 20 years ago. Harvard's classrooms have many more design features than suggested by this figure. What is important for this presentation is that each student has a reasonable chance to see and hear each other student, as well as an unrestricted view of the professor and the chalkboard or other visual displays in the front of the room. The teacher can move about in the "pit", the floor area in front of the first rows of seats, and even move up the aisles among the other seats.

Figure 7 An effective classroom layout for case method

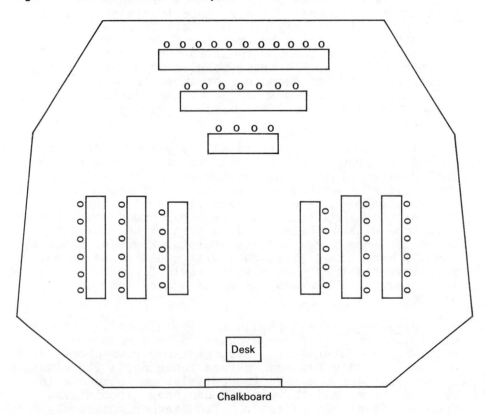

116

It would be a mistake to suggest that case method teaching cannot go on in a classroom less elaborately adapted to the method.   In fact, most case method teachers have adapted themselves to far less ideal class-rooms.   Where it is possible to rearrange the seating, one should set up the class either in one large "U" (effective with up to 25 students) or two tiers.   If it is not possible to elevate the rear tiers, it may be necessary to elevate the chalkboard and the teacher's desk or lectern.   What is important is to set up the classroom to facilitate eye contact between the teacher and each student and, so far as possible, among students.

Visual aids and acoustics are critically important to case method teaching.   In earlier chapters the teacher's use of the chalkboard as an integral part of the inter-active teaching of case method was stressed. The quality and size of the chalkboard are important. Furthermore, the lighting in the room must allow all students to see what is on the chalkboard without glare. The distance and angle of all seats in relation to the chalkboard is an important design criterion for new classroom installations.   If every student is to be able to hear each other student's recitation, acoustics also must be checked.

In existing buildings, and particularly when one is establishing a short programme in a hotel or other rented facility, substantially less ideal circumstances must be accommodated to.   When the only room you can use for a classroom is the wrong size or shape, the lighting is poor and the acoustics terrible, you must adapt by adjust-ing the size of your class, the class timetable and other variables within the teacher's control.

Other useful visual aids, in the best of all poss-ible worlds, include screens which pull down in front of the chalkboard for use with overhead projectors, slide and motion picture projectors.   Audio systems for use with sound films and tape cassettes are useful.   Imagina-tive use can be made of television recording equipment, as well.   None of these is essential to support case method, however.   The chalkboard is essential.

Potential for case selection
and duplication

In many industrialised countries an institution can foster case method teaching and rely on other institu-tions to provide case materials.   The same is not true in the developing world.   Probably most case teaching in the western countries is conducted using published case books.   Arrangements to have these available are no more difficult than the arrangements for having textbooks available. As has been pointed out, however, case books specifically designed for use in developing countries are rare. Loose-leaf cases, and particularly newly written cases dealing with the problems of each region, are likely to be the answer for many institutions. And such arrangements require special adaptations. The special problems of a case clearing-house are described more fully in Chapter 14. What is detailed here is primarily the needs of a single institution which is adopting cases.

Cases that are ordered from a clearing-house require a facility for storage and retrieval on demand. As soon as three or four teachers in different courses are using cases regularly it is probably time to centralise the process of ordering and receiving cases, if only to provide for budgetary controls. Although it is best, the author believes, to file cases in the order of the issuing clearing-house's identification numbers, one needs also a cross-reference file by case name. In order to facilitate the transfer of responsibility for a course from one teacher to another, an institution's case librarian should keep a copy of each year's syllabus for every case course, giving the order of use of cases by name and identification number.

When loose-leaf cases are used, one of the strengths of case method is the facility with which the teacher can change a single case in the next year's syllabus. What constitutes facility for the teacher, however, can prove to be a headache for the librarian. Whereas with a case book or a textbook it is only necessary to keep track of a single item to support the next year's syllabus, with loose-leaf cases it may be a matter of 30 or 40 different items. The problem of "dead stock" can be severe, if advance notice is not given when a teacher plans to change the syllabus. Yet it would be inappropriate for the librarian to control the teacher by requiring a rigid adherence to exactly the original list of cases. Perhaps it is enough to suggest that an effective inventory control system should be adopted from the beginning. If each teacher is held responsible in some way for a budget for teaching materials, it should help avoid waste. Yet the budget must be sufficient for the teacher to order and reproduce enough cases, or the whole system will be defeated.

When teachers at the institution begin writing cases for themselves, the case "librarian's" job becomes more complicated. Assisting teachers in getting cases typed and duplicated, adding new identification numbers to cases, and particularly keeping up with editorial changes from case draft to case draft are among the tasks that must be faced. Many institutions have mimeograph (or cyclostyle) duplication capabilities. With such machines, the decision about how many copies to run from the first is a difficult one to make. There is always a trade-off between the relatively cheap extra copies being run on the first pass and the cost of keeping finished cases in stock for a year or two. The risk of obsolescence is high, as well. A teacher may make so many changes in a case between the first and second uses that the case must be entirely retyped.

Some institutions have the capability of making a "Ditto" master by a thermal process from a typed original. This is often a very attractive solution to the problem of retaining enough copies. The library can retain a typed "master" copy of the case, and include with it, if desired, the "Ditto" masters if they have not already been used to their capacity. Then only the desired number of copies for each use need be run off. Changes in the case can more easily be made in the typed master copies.

One of the most expensive ways to provide copies is by making direct photocopies. Although this is often the easiest and quickest way to make a few copies, it is far too expensive to be considered as the primary way to provide multiple copies for students' use.

A question that needs to be answered is how the budget for loose-leaf cases is to be met. In some institutions the students are expected to pay something extra, above tuition, for textbooks. At such places, it is important to establish the principle that loose-leaf cases and notes are in the nature of textbook materials, else the budgetary comparisons between case method and other teaching methods will be unnecessarily worsened. In other institutions course fees may include a provision for the purchase of case materials. Even where no charge is made for textbooks, as case method is introduced it is well to keep track of case costs in an account like a "textbook" account. If the costs are merely buried in the office or library operating costs, the shock to the budget-watchers may be great.

One final element enters into the job of safe-keeping cases. Often a teacher holds back one or more cases for use as examination cases. If students can find a key to the case coding system so that they know which cases are dedicated to a particular course, they are often ingenious enough to forecast what cases will become exams. If copies of such cases are "around", from previous years' use or through lower-level library employees, an exam scandal might result. Provisions must therefore be made for safekeeping of syllabi as well

as the cases themselves.   And where a teacher is saving
one of his/her own cases for a future exam, those who
type and duplicate the case must be trusted and specially
trained.   One way to keep unauthorised distribution of
cases to a minimum is to insist on exact counts from
duplicator runs, and to destroy any imperfect sheets or
extra copies beyond those called for by the print order.

Case writing potential

To write cases calls for more than mere interest
and dedication on the part of the teacher.   Case writing
takes time.   It takes a modest amount of money for
expenses.   It takes recognition when the job is well
done.   And it requires some administrative support in
the way of record-keeping and the like.

Time is probably the most critical need, and one
which is most often lacking.   Where case writing is to
be fostered, the institution's management learns to know
just how much time is required to develop the cases for
a new segment of a course, for example, and is willing to
factor into a teacher's schedule the time needed to do
so.   Even where it is not possible to reduce a teacher's
number of classroom hours, it is often possible to reduce
the load of committee and quasi-administrative work
required of a teacher who has an ambitious case writing
schedule.   If the teacher must do case writing entirely
on his/her own time, then at least the case writing must
receive recognition as a highly professional activity,
or it will not be done.

Money for expenses is often overlooked.   Not much
field research can be conducted on the campus.   Sometimes the site for an excellent case will be in another
city.   To adopt "case method" and provide nothing for it
its support in the budget is self-defeating.   Of course,
the costs of secretarial help, duplicating and storing
cases have been mentioned above;   they are not to be
ignored.

Other support includes recognition for case writing,
more fully covered in a later chapter, and a system for
keeping track of the various case writing activities of
a number of teachers.   So long as the case writing is
being done by a handful of teachers at an institution,
and so long as all the teachers know each other and keep
reasonably in touch, no formal record-keeping is necessary, although it might even then be useful.   But as
soon as the numbers of case writers exceed about ten, and
when they are all actively pursuing case writing, some
form of central registry becomes necessary, to avoid over-
lap and embarrassment in the contacts made by the writers.

For example, faculty member X may have been carefully developing a case lead with the President of the
Delta Corporation, in the hope of writing a series of
cases about the company. Because he was in the first
stages of the contact, he would not generally be talking
openly with all his colleagues about his plans. Some
might know about it, but not all. Suppose that a
junior colleague catches a "target of opportunity" with
the Delta Corporation. His friend, the personnel
manager may give him a little case dealing with a knotty
problem of disciplinary action. When that case is
finished and released, a copy may lie in Delta's files,
where it is brought to the attention of the President.
Although he may not be upset at the smaller case having
been released, at least he may feel that his role as a
benefactor of case method teaching has been undermined.

Other examples could easily be drawn from the
experiences of case writers the world over. The values
of a central contact file are severalfold. By identifying organisations that are known to co-operate with
case writers, and noting the faculty member who has the
best contacts, the file facilitates opening doors for
young faculty about to write their first cases. By
"blocking" organisations that are being worked to their
capacity at the moment they avoid embarrassing over-
contacts. And by letting the new faculty member know
which older faculty to talk to about contacts, they can
help the institution avoid adverse criticism by not
repeating past mistakes. Finally, of course, when a
reference to a comprehensive case contact file shows no
previous contact with a company, it clears the road for
a new researcher to make a contact.

One problem exists with such central case contact
files, however. They are difficult to keep complete
and up to date. Some faculty members are dilatory in
reporting their contacts and their completions. It is
not always easy to know when a "contact" has been made.
It is wasteful for a selfish faculty member to "block"
contacts with four companies he/she hopes to contact
soon. And when two faculty members seem to make simultaneous contacts with different parts of the same firm
it is not clear how one should establish priorities.
All such administrative problems are endurable, however.
They do not obviate the desirability of setting up such
a file.

Introducing cases in the teaching process

In most institutions, the decision to enhance the
use of cases in teaching management and administration

cannot be implemented within a few days.   This applies
in particular to courses that have been taught for some
time by traditional methods.   Introducing cases in such
courses may be a somewhat tricky operation, and yet one
that is entirely useful to try.   The problems arise
from two sources.   First, many students who have learned
mostly by lecture method and reading are so unused to
participating actively in class that they do not gain
all the benefits of case method.   Second, teachers who
are used only to lecturing tend to be so impatient with
students during a case method class that they lapse back
into "lecturing about the case", and the special value
of case method is again lost sight of.   When so few
cases are used that the students never learn to talk and
the teacher never learns to keep quiet, cases are at best
"examples", and the lecture method continues to overwhelm
the case method.

With experience, however, good cases can be added
to lecture courses.   One way to do this is to have the
lecturer share the classroom with an experienced case
method teacher on the days when cases are being discussed.
Not all institutions foster an environment where this is
possible, but if it is not threatening to the lecturer,
it can work very well.   The very fact that another
teacher is standing before the room forces the students
to pay attention to new cues.   The experienced case
method teacher can keep quiet long enough for the students to think out what to say, and so on.

Another way to use cases in lecture courses is to
assign a case to a group of students to prepare and make
a presentation to the rest of the class.   When the
teacher sits down, he/she is less likely to overwhelm
student participation.   A series of such assignments
might be enough to give every student a chance to participate in a group analysis and presentation of a case.

A skilful use of the case method is particularly
important to short seminars and other programmes,
organised for managers with practical experience.   In
these instances, the ideas of subject-matter, clientele
and duration of programme arise concurrently.   All three
variables will affect the choice of cases.   Among participants who are preselected and preregistered for a
programme, it is possible to send the first day's cases
in advance, so that the programme can start from the
first sessions with case discussions.   A far more usual
circumstance is that the programme starts without prior
preparation by the participants.   In such instances, it
is necessary to start the programme with cases which can
be read and discussed within the time allotted for the
sessions, i.e. short cases selected with due regard to
the level of participants' knowledge and experience and

to their motivations and expectations. Such cases provide an excellent opening to programmes focusing on practical issues common to a number of managers.

Apart from the difficulty surrounding the first day, design criteria for short case method programmes are similar to those mentioned in other parts of this manual for longer courses. In general, one does less experimenting with new cases in short programmes. Also, one builds in less redundancy in short programmes than in longer courses. Each case should have a very precise teaching purpose. Post-experience participants often fall easily into the habits required by case method if the programme director is consistent in encouraging preparation and active participation.

It should be mentioned again that more active discussion and a wider variety of insight from experience is to be expected from post-experience programme participants than from university students. It is especially important, therefore, that teachers who lead such programmes should themselves have wide experience both in teaching and in case writing.

The use of cases is particularly appropriate in in-company (internal) training of managers and supervisors. In large organisations it is often possible to have cases written directly from the files of the organisation involved, so that training can be geared not only to typical problems encountered in the organisation but also to practices and procedures. Usually it is good to disguise the individuals involved in such "internal" cases, even if it can be known rather easily by many participants where the incidents occurred. There is no need to create embarrassment for anyone even when cases can easily be written and released for internal use.

In countries where there are no large companies, jointly sponsored case method training programmes can be developed, in which a number of non-competing companies establish training programmes for managers and supervisors. Management institutions can help to design and organise such programmes involving groups of companies. Here, also, cases can be used as a training medium. The author believes, however, that for such programmes cases should be developed with all the special attention to disguise that is suggested for cases to be used in external courses at universities and management institutions.

In deciding to use cases, the teacher will be well advised to consider the benefits of alternative teaching and training methods not merely in general terms, but in the relationship to a specific learning situation. For example, if the subject to be covered is "company mergers" and has to be presented to a group of senior general managers, the teacher may be in a position to give a lecture, recommend individual reading, use one or more written cases, organise one or more role-playing exercises, arrange discussions with managers of companies that have been merged and so on. A choice is to be made and it is not possible to give a universal guideline on what this choice should be.[1]

All in all, when preparing any of the programmes mentioned in this section the teacher has to consider what method is most likely to be effective in achieving a particular learning objective with a particular group of participants. In addition, he has to consider what case and other training material is available or can be prepared before the programme starts, how many course sessions will be at his disposal and to what sort of teaching and group-work are most participants used. He will then establish his teaching strategy for the programme, and in many instances (e.g. if he is a junior teacher, if several teachers contribute to the same programme or if the programme is important) this teaching strategy will be discussed with other people at the institution to reach collective consensus on the direction to follow. The issue is important enough to warrant full attention of those who are responsible for the institution's policy and strategy.

---

[1] See, e.g. M. Kubr "Principles for selection of teaching and training methods" in ILO: An introductory course in teaching and training methods for management development (Geneva, International Labour Office, 1972).

CASEWRITERS' WORKSHOPS

13

Case writing is a skill.   As a skill, it can be
learned, and is best learned, by guided practice.   For
many years case writers have been developed and trained
by case method teachers on a "one-on-one" basis, and this
is still a prevalent mode.   Especially when case writers
are recent graduates of management degree programmes,
working for teachers at institutions where case method is
well established, the one-on-one method is excellent.
But it is slow.   When there are too few experienced
case writing teachers in a region, and recent graduates
of degree programmes are themselves in high demand as
executives and teachers, some means must be found to
train a "critical mass" of teachers in case writing
skills, looking forward to the day when each institution
may have an ongoing case writing programme.   The "case
writers' workshop" has evolved to help develop this
critical mass.   The story of the first 11 workshops,
directed by Andrew R. Towl of the Harvard Business School
is well described in literature.[1]

Case writing workshops have been offered under various auspices around the world, usually led by people who
have themselves had previous case writing and workshop
experience.   Although the leading of case writers' workshops, like so much of case method, must be learned by
doing, it is possible to suggest a number of guidelines
for the operation, based on experience with the technique.
These suggestions follow, under the general headings of
sponsorship, location, clientele, structure and duration,
content and conduct, and general instructions.
Appendix 12 contains sample materials for use in organising a workshop.

---

[1] See Andrew R. Towl: <u>To study administration by
cases</u> (Boston, Harvard University, 1969).

Sponsorship

The need for sponsorship arises for two reasons.
Case writer's workshops are expensive, and it is highly
unlikely that tuition charges can be made sufficiently
high to defray the expenses. Secondly, workshops
require a great deal of preplanning. Therefore some
institution must provide "advance men" to set things up.
Sometimes, of course, the same institution will provide
both money and participants for the workshops. This
will no doubt often be the pattern when a single institution is large enough to mount a workshop exclusively
for its own teachers or trainers.

No general rule can be set forth concerning the
cost of a workshop. Cost depends too much on the
country of location, the number of participants, the
duration of the programme and other design variables
that cannot be specified in advance. It is, however,
possible to define certain costs as fixed and others as
variable, so that effective plans can be made once the
costs of specific items become known. Thinking in
terms of fixed and variable costs also helps to decide
what costs might well be borne by the sponsor and what
charged to the participants.

Major fixed costs (costs which do not vary with the
number of participants) include salary and expenses of
the workshop leader, the workshop administrative assistant and the workshop secretary, rent for the workshop
facilities and the "front money", or the cost of
announcements and promotion for the workshop. Each of
these types of cost can be influenced greatly by the
strategy for organising the workshop. If the workshop
leader travels a long distance and must be housed in a
hotel, his/her expenses can even exceed the professional
fees. At the other extreme, an "in-house" workshop
leader, conducting a workshop in his/her home city and
carrying the administrative responsibility as well as
the leadership responsibility for the workshop, represents far less out-of-pocket cost.

Major variable costs (costs which vary in total
amount depending upon the number of participants) are
the salaries of participants, participants' travel and
living expenses, programme supplies such as copies of
cases and notes, and the salaries and expenses of participants during their case writing efforts. Not only do
these costs vary in total amount depending upon the
number of participants, but they also differ substantially among participants. Once again, the strategy of programme design can influence greatly the amount of these
costs.

126

If any workshop costs can be shifted from the sponsor to the participants or the participants' employers, variable costs are easiest to shift. In virtually every instance the participants' employers bear the salary costs, although the author knows of some examples of participants who have attended workshops during vacation periods. Participants' employers usually bear the costs of case writing expenses, and often the travel and living expenses of participants during workshop meetings. Sometimes a "tuition" fee is charged, to help defray the fixed expenses of the programme.

So many variants of sponsorship and clientele are possible that it would be foolish to generalise further. In planning a workshop, responsible administrators must estimate the above costs, fixed and variable, as carefully as possible. Attempts to minimise or shift the incidence of the costs must then be contemplated as a part of the over-all strategy for the workshop. Each of the following design features of workshops has a budgetary implication as well as a potential affect on the quality of the programme.

Workshop location (venue)

There are effective arguments both for and against locating a workshop meeting away from the normal workplace of participants. The principal argument for "getting away from the office" is to avoid the intrusion of day-to-day operations into the workshop activities. Against this benefit must be measured the additional cost of travel and accommodation expenses for participants.

When a workshop serves participants from several institutions, of course, many will have to leave their home base in any event. In such an instance it is desirable to site the programme in a place where none of the participants need to feel that they must play hosts to the others. The group solidarity that is fostered by sharing a common experience away from home makes a positive contribution to the success of a workshop.

A case writers' workshop should be sited in a city where active industries are located. An isolated "retreat" is not appropriate. Nearby industrial units make possible the factory visits that are an important activity of the workshop. Furthermore, if active case writing is to be undertaken while the workshop is in progress, co-operating organisations in the area are even more essential.

A second requisite for the workshop location is a
training or conference centre thet offers an appropriate
meeting room and other case method facilities.   The
advance party should see the room and facilities being
offered, and make these an important part of the choice
of venue.   Often major difficulties surround acoustics,
room layout and lighting.   Very infrequently, in developing countries, does a hotel have chalkboard facilities of
the size and quality to facilitate a good case discussion.
In fact, hotel managers seldom recognise the special needs
for inter-active discussion meetings.   If they are set
up for speeches and banquets, they see no reason why they
don't have "excellent facilities for training".

Having living accommodation and meeting rooms close
enough together that participants can walk between them
is highly desirable.   In short programmes it is too
costly to have to wait even a quarter of an hour past
the starting time for laggards to make their way through
traffic from their hotel to a remote meeting room site.

Clientele

It is feasible to design case writing workshops
along several lines.   One could restrict the workshop to
participants from a single large institution.   One could
admit participants from a variety of institutions, but
restrict the content of the workshop to a single discipline (e.g. accounting or human behaviour).   Each definition of the programme that restricts the clientele will
have an effect on the contents and structure of the programme.   The description that follows assumes a minimum
of restrictions on clientele.   Participants may come
from different disciplines, from different institutions,
institutions of different sorts, and even from other
countries, so long as common language can be used.
Although it is possible to teach a case method class
through simultaneous translators, the difficulties in
teaching case writing in this way would be enormous.

Particularly in developing countries, the benefits
from offering workshops to the broadest possible clientele
are great.   Few universities and management institutions
have enough faculty members who need such instruction to
be able to fill the rolls of a programme.   There are
positive benefits beyond the case writing efforts themselves to bring faculty members of different institutions
together.   The inclusion of training directors from
public and private enterprises should be encouraged, the
author believes.   Such persons bring an additional touch
of realism into the discussions.

It is useful to require that participants detail in
advance the amount of prior exposure they have had to
case method.   Prior teaching experience using cases is
useful, but not essential to success in the workshop
design shown here.   Only if one were to design a shorter
programme, such prior experience might be necessary.
The author prefers participants to have had some teaching
or training experience, but even this is not absolutely
necessary for every participant.   It is highly desirable
that participants foresee that they will be encouraged
to write and use cases once they return to their institutions, but experience has shown that in many areas of the
world such expectations cannot be guaranteed.

Structure and duration

There are two major designs for workshops, with many
minor variations.   One major design has the participants
coming together for a single period of time, during
which all activities of the workshop are completed,
including writing each participant's first case.   This
was, in fact, the design of the prototype workshops at
Harvard.   Such workshops occupied eight weeks of intensive and well-supervised activity.   They were an
acclaimed success.   The author believes, however, that
it would be extremely expensive if not impossible to
duplicate the special circumstances that made available
to those workshops abundant human resources both of
clientele and of leadership.   It is worth listing the
resources that accompanied those successful efforts:

- an outstanding and experienced workshop leader;

- a number of experienced case method teachers and
  case writers to act as "coaches" for small groups
  of participants;

- ideal case method teaching facilities;

- living accommodations immediately adjacent to the
  teaching facilities;

- an abundance of co-operating industrial leaders who
  offered case writing sites, with contacts established in advance;

- excellent secretarial and duplicating facilities;
  and, not least,

- a generally experienced group of participants.

The author believes that the second major workshop
structure, which might be called a "sandwich programme"

is more feasible in most instances.   The following
description, therefore, is in terms of a sandwich programme, i.e. a programme where a workshop is held for a
three-week period (phase 1), followed by several months
of individual case writing efforts by participants
(phase 2) and concluding with an intensive final workshop (phase 3) where the new cases are examined.   This
structure has several advantages over the single-period
workshop, especially for programmes involving participants from different regions or countries.   Aside from
obvious savings in variable costs the sandwich programme
requires participants to develop case leads in their own
regions, which is a far more realistic environment for
case writing than are the pre-established case contacts
in the region where the workshop is held.

The duration of a workshop depends upon several
factors.   As will be seen, the first phase of the workshop has the dual purpose of introducing a number of
concepts about case method, case teaching and case writing and of giving participants some experience in using
the method.   In circumstances where all participants
were experienced case method teachers the second purpose
could be minimised.   If the participants are few in
number, the experiences of teaching require fewer sessions.   If the workshop is to serve 10 to 15 participants, 3 weeks is about right for the first phase of the
programme.   The duration of the middle portion of the
programme is often determined by the length of teaching
terms or semesters at institutions in the region.   That
is, the first phase is scheduled to come during the long
break between teaching terms, and the third phase during
the next following short break.   The third phase must
be long enough for every participant who has prepared a
case to conduct a discussion of his/her new case, benefit
from comments from other participants, and prepare a rewritten version of the case.   Usually this can be done
during a period about as many working days long as there
are returning participants, if the whole group works
together.   If it were impossible to schedule this many
days, it would be best to schedule about one half day
per case, and to divide the group into separate working
parties to assist in going over the finally rewritten
cases.   The inherent implications for the duration of
sessions will emerge as each of the elements of content
is discussed in the following paragraphs.

Content and conduct

The content of the first phase of a workshop cannot
be specified in detail, lacking knowledge of the number
and experience level of participants.   It is, however,
possible to describe seven major activities of a typical

130

workshop. The amount of time devoted to each can vary considerably, depending on the workshop leader's understanding of the needs of the particular group. The activities and their purposes are as follows:

1. <u>Case discussions and feedback</u> occupy more sessions than any other activity. Such discussions serve the major purpose of giving each participant at least one experience of leading a case discussion followed by feedback from the group. These sessions serve at least two subsidiary purposes, as well. They acquaint participants with specific cases that may prove useful later on, and they provide a series of common experiences for the whole group. These common experiences, to which the workshop leader can refer when appropriate, tend to illustrate nearly every facet of case method.

After the first four case discussion sessions directed by the workshop leader, each of the cases is led by a different participant until every participant has had at least one such experience. The first hour or so of a 1 3/4 to 2 hour class should be devoted to the discussion of the case, with the avowed purpose of arriving at a solution to the case problem itself. Usually the workshop leader should try to match cases and case leaders, so that a quantitative case is led by a quantitatively oriented teacher, a marketing case by a marketing instructor, and so on. This suggests that there should be available for the workshop a somewhat larger number of cases than the leader expects to use, to allow for selection.

Criteria for case selection, other than matching cases to participants' skills and interests, are as follows. The first two cases, which occur on the first day, must be short enough to be studied and discussed within a class period. Usually one of these is qualitatively oriented and the other quantitatively oriented. A case in human relations, with few numbers in it, serves well for the former. A marketing case which includes some tables relating sales by month or a simple case giving sales and cost data for a small firm would serve well for the latter. The important part about the first two cases is to choose examples that yield rather readily to common sense analytical approaches. This makes it easy for the workshop leader to ensure that every participant has a rewarding experience of speaking up in the discussion.

In general, cases grow larger, more complex and more specialised as the programme goes on. The workshop leader must realise, however, that this discussion is the first one many participants have ever led. It is a good idea, therefore, to stay away from the most complicated

cases entirely, in a workshop of this length. However,
if two or three cases are available of varying levels of
complexity, but drawing on a single analytical technique,
it is useful to expose the students to them all, in
order to have a chance to refer to the way in which they
"build" on one another. A final criterion is that
cases and notes represent a range of the types identified
in Chapter 9.

The last part of each period should be devoted to a
"feedback" session, during which the participants revert
to the roles of teachers from the roles they played as
"students" during the discussions. This part of the
period should raise and answer questions such as the
following, with the feedback sessions led by a participant other than the one who led the case discussion:

- What were the teaching purposes of the case and of
  the discussion leader?

- How effective was the case in supporting these
  purposes?

- How might this case be used in teaching in your
  country or institution? In what curricula?
  In what specific courses? For what level of
  students?

- Could a case be developed in your country which
  would deal with the same topic, while being more
  relevant and easier to understand for students
  in this environment?

Notice that the feedback sessions do not specifically
criticise the skill of the session leader. Occasionally
some perceptive questions may help the discussion leader
to see how he/she could improve teaching style, but this
is not a central purpose of these workshops. It can be
very discouraging to participants if criticism becomes
the main point of the feedback sessions.

Case discussions and feedback sessions will occupy
as many sessions as there are participants, plus two to
four sessions led by the workshop leader, one each led
by any "coaches" involved in the programme, and one or
more by each "guest teacher" who participates in the programme by invitation.

2. "Concept-oriented" sessions fill those gaps that
cannot be handled directly by cases. Some of these
sessions will consist of discussions of readings, some
of lectures, and some of special exercises. A sample
list of concepts that the workshop leader may want to
emphasise appears in the typical programme format

132

suggested in later paragraphs.   In general, the agenda
for these sessions follows the format of this manual,
focusing on case method and the student, case method and
the teacher, case writing, and case method in the institution.   These sessions, which may go best in the after-
noons, leaving the mornings for case discussions, will
constitute less than 25% of the typical workshop.

To the extent that it is possible, these sessions
should involve inter-action among students, even if they
are not based upon cases.   An example of such an inter-
active exercise is reported in Chapter 7, where the
analogy between a stone wall and course development concepts is explained.   After reading that chapter and
discussing briefly the nature of the analogy, students
break into small groups (called "syndicates" in some
countries) to develop their own "building blocks" for
their courses.   In this instance it is valuable for the
small groups to consist as much as possible of persons
from the same discipline.

The next three activities provide experience in the
data-gathering and case writing process.

3.   Factory visits and related discussions.   Each
workshop should contain at least two and preferably three
factory visits.   The factories visited should differ
from one another as much as possible, offering a range of
size and differing technologies.   Each factory should
occupy three class periods of the workshop.   One period,
of about two hours, is usually sufficient for the visit
itself (particularly if it is scheduled in the afternoon,
which is the preferred time).   A second period should
be set aside for small groups to meet to discuss what
they have seen on the visit, and to prepare a presentation about their observations.   The third period provides
time for a spokesperson for each group to present the
group's findings and submit to questions about it.   Each
small group may be given the same charge, such as "keep
your eyes open for things you believe would lead to good
case writing", or each group may be assigned a different
aspect of the situation to which to pay particular attention.   If time is available, part of a session prior to
the factory visit can be devoted to discussing and pre-
planning for each visit.

The purposes for these factory visits are to allow
participants to have the experience of identifying or
finding cases in the field and to practise observation
and note taking.   Often the groups may be able to interview a responsible executive, which leads to experience
in interviewing.   A variant of the report-back procedure
is to invite a representative of the company to be
present when the groups present their reports.   If this

is planned, it is a good idea for the workshop leader to hear a preliminary version of the group reports. This will take more time, but it interjects an added element of realism which acts as an incentive for many participants.

4. "One-on-one" interview exercise. Because a great deal of the data-gathering of field cases is done by interviews, a specific interviewing experience is useful. Assign participants to teams of two, allowing self-selection of pairs a few days after the workshop starts. Avoid getting two persons from the same institution in the same team. Each member of a pair is then instructed to interview the other in an attempt to gather sufficient information to write a case about some managerial or professional experience the other person has undergone. Either a full morning or a full afternoon should be devoted to the interviews.

Each participant then writes up the "case" gathered as a result of the interviews. One full session's worth of time should be set aside for this writing. Ideally, one might assign a Friday morning to interviews, Friday afternoon to writing, and then be prepared for presentations the following Monday. This allows slower writers to use some of their own time on the week-end if necessary.

If good secretarial service is available to the workshop, each participant's case drawn from the interviews would be typed, duplicated and handed out to other participants prior to the discussion sessions. Failing this, each interviewer gives a detailed oral presentation of his/her case. Following the presentation, the person interviewed is asked, "would you release the case as presented, or would you like to see some changes?" This provides for some mild and non-threatening feedback to the writer about how well he/she has listened during the interview. This may then be followed by a short general discussion of each case, kept brief enough so that four to six cases can be presented in each class period.

5. Research using other data sources. In countries where corporations' annual reports are generally available, it is useful to spend one or more sessions in examining and analysing annual reports. The purpose of such activity is to identify possible cases that might be found at the subject companies. Other sources that could be followed up in addition to or in place of company annual reports are corporate public relations releases, newspaper accounts of business activity and research in the business periodicals and books available in a local institutional library.

134

Once again, it is imperative for participants to have time to do the research and to have their ideas tested in front of their peers. It would be inappropriate to schedule this research activity without providing time for feedback.

6. "How-to-do-it" sessions. At least two or three class sessions should be devoted to reviewing, step by step, the process of case writing. Each participant should be given an opportunity to ask questions and express his/her doubts and fears about the process. Usually some other member of the group will have an answer to nearly every question that may be raised. The workshop leader, however, will need to be confident enough to counter the fear that "case writing can never be started in my country because ...".

Much of the substance of the "how-to" sessions should be in the form of extended examples of the case writing process. Each workshop leader can help in the development of future workshops by collecting and writing up the experiences of his/her participants, as case histories.

7. Individual discussions between participants and the workshop leader. Towards the end of the first phase of the workshop, the leader should schedule an evening meeting of at least an hour with each participant, to hear his/her plans for conducting case research. The major purpose of these interviews is to give the participants a sense of commitment to writing a case. Mainly by asking questions about the participants' case leads, the leader can help the participant foresee some of the problems each case lead might present. At this time, also, the leader can discover whether a participant has misunderstood any of the major points of the planned case writing exercise. In the extreme case of someone who finds it very difficult to conceive of writing a case, the leader can assist in organising the participant's search for a case lead.

The rough proportions of the above activities in a three-week programme with three formal class sessions per day is as follows:

- case discussions and feedback   20-25 sessions
- concept-oriented sessions   6-10   "
- factory visits and related   6- 9   "
- interviews and related   4- 6   "
- other data source research   2- 4   "
- "how-to" sessions   2- 3   "
- individual discussions   (outside of class time)

Total sessions   45

The conduct of _the second phase_ of the workshop,
when participants return to their home bases to undertake
case writing efforts, depends largely upon resources of
the workshop, both human and monetary. If the workshop
leader can travel to visit the participants during this
period, it will help considerably, since the schedule for
his/her arrivals can act as a prod for activity. If
graduates of previous case writing programmes can be
called upon for assistance in this process, it is useful.
Otherwise, at least there should be correspondence between the leader or administrative assistants and all
participants to encourage activity. It is often useful
to set an intermediate deadline, such as the requirement
that a "first draft" of a case be forwarded a month or
two before the start of the third phase. Every effort
should be made to keep the enthusiasm high through this
period when the participants are on their own.

The third phase of the workshop focuses upon the
participants' new cases and teaching notes. No other
new content is introduced. The procedure should be for
the author of a case to lead the other participants in a
discussion of the case, just as it would be used in class.
The time for this discussion should not exceed a normal
class period, and during this discussion the workshop
leader should keep quiet, except for intervening to keep
participants from deserting their roles as "students".

Immediately following the discussion of the case
problem, the workshop leader can step in to direct a discussion of how the case might be improved. This session
might well start by a statement from the case author,
indicating how he/she reacted to the participants' discussion of the case. If the author has prepared a
preliminary teaching note, it should be distributed at
this time. Usually all that can be done by other
participants during this discussion is to seek clarification of parts of the case that the group has misinterpre-
ted and suggest inclusion of some additional information.

The role of the workshop leader in this session can
be far more ambitious. As an experienced field
researcher, he/she can often identify more in a case than
the author and participants have thought of. In one
instance an author had written an excellent case for his
marketing course. Its purpose was to show how to decide
on product line changes because of relative sales figures.
The exhibits he presented with the case were in sufficient
detail to allow the case to be used in studying relative
pricing decisions and contribution margins. These other
analyses made the case interesting for use by teachers of
accounting and control as well as marketing.

After the author of a case has had the benefit of the group's comments, he/she should modify the case while the third phase is in session, if at all possible. The workshop secretary can then provide the author with a new clean draft to use for obtaining a formal release. The sponsors of the workshop should follow up to be sure that the release is actually obtained.[1]

Although a case writer will prepare better teaching notes after having taught a case several times to regular students, it is worth while for the workshop leader to insist that a preliminary teaching note be prepared before or during the third phase of the workshop. Preparing a teaching note is an extremely useful device to force the case writer to understand his/her own case and its various potential uses.

Also during phase three, workshop leaders should pay attention to the stories told by participants about their experiences in all aspects of case writing. Some of these experiences are worth writing is case histories, which can become the media for introducing a next generation of case writers to the process.

A typical workshop programme

The programme for phase 1 of a workshop that was held at the Centre for Management Development in Nigeria in 1978 is given below. Most of the cases were from non-Nigerian sources. Three coaches returned from a workshop held the previous year. The cases they taught were ones they themselves had written. One guest teacher was available. Because he was an expert in human relations, and particularly experienced in non-directive interviewing techniques, his sessions were devoted to two appraisal cases and a concept session dealing with interviewing techniques. The programme did not include research from published sources, but otherwise contained all elements of the seven activities suggested above. The author followed the practice of issuing each week's timetable on Friday of the week before, which allowed some of the activities to be arranged for even while the programme was going on. This was necessary because factory visits and the arrival dates for guest teachers and coaches could not be determined very far in advance.

Most of the cases and reading used in the Nigerian programme are available from the ICCH.[2] This manual

---

[1] See Chapter 10 for details.

[2] See Appendix 14.

covers the same ground as the readings, and several
cases are made available with this manual, with suggestions about where they might be used in a workshop.
Each workshop leader, however, should feel comfortable
in selecting cases from the local context, if they are
available, and supplementing them by further cases of
his choice as appropriate.

First week

Monday	1	Formal opening	Director of the Centre
	2	Case: Gordon Foundry	Workshop leader (WL)
	3	Case: Gentle Electric	Coach (C)
Tuesday	1	Case: Dasham Co.	WL
	2	Case: Rennett Machine	WL
	3	Concept discussion based on readings: "How to study a case" and "Because wisdom can't be told"	
Wednesday	1	Case: Crown Fastener	Participant (P)
	2	Case: Weston Manufac- turing	P
	3	Concept discussion based on "Managerial problem solving and the case method"	
Thursday	1	Case: Lamson Co.	C
	2	Case: Vine Dairy	P
	3	Concept discussion based on "Use of case material in the class- room"	
Friday	1	Case: Superior Slate Quarry	P
	2	Case: Jason Supply	P
	3	Concept discussion "Cases which meet the student's needs" and lecture on field research	

Second week

Monday	1 Case: John Edwards	P
	2 Case: Allen Co.	P
	3 Concept discussion: Organising ideas, "building blocks" of courses	
Tuesday	1 Case: The Case of the Missing Time	P
	2 Case: Broadside Boat	P
	3 Concept discussion: "Course development"	
Wednesday	1 Case: Ashok Rajguru	Guest leader (G)
	2 Case: Hart and Bing, basis for role playing	G
	3 Concept discussion: Non-directive interview- ing techniques	G
Thursday	1 Case: Atkins and Wexler	P
	2 Preparation for factory visit	
	3 Factory visit: National Tobacco Company	
Friday	1 Syndicates report back on factory visit	
	2 Preparation for inter- view exercise	
	3 Interview exercise	

Third week

Monday	1 Case: Shaldon and Sons	P
	2 Case: Blitz Company	P
	3 Concept discussion: "Writing business cases"	
Tuesday	1 Discussion of "cases" arising from interview exercise	
	2 Discussion of "cases" arising from interview exercise	
	3 Lecture and discussion: "How to write cases in Nigeria"	

Wednesday	1	Preparation for factory visit	
	2	Factory visit: plastics factory	
	3	Case: Ekpo Family Enterprises	C
Thursday	1	Syndicates report back on factory visit	
	2	Case: Unity Furniture	C
	3	Concept discussion: "Case development and the teaching note"	
Friday	1	Case: Voltamp Electrical Corp.	WL
	2	Discussion of how to improve the case "Bert Angeles"	WL
	3	Closing ceremonies	

General instructions

There are a few other useful instructions that have to be considered at this point.

The workshop leader will find it useful, if experienced case writers are available, to have one of them working with each five or six inexperienced participants. During the workshop the leader will often want to have the participants break into small groups, and having one experienced person to assign to each group as a coach is very helpful. Each leader should define the role of the coach as appropriate to the situation. One good source of coaches is the most successful case writers from a previous workshop. Assigning these people as coaches gives them a chance to meet and influence the next group of participants. When coaches are used, they should lead case discussions early in the first phase of the workshop, to let them get acquainted with participants.

When there are no experienced coaches, the workshop should be limited to 12-15 participants, since the leader will need to supply all the expertise at every juncture.

If "guest teachers" who are expert in case method can be brought in once or twice during phase one, this is useful. The workshop leader will find his/her face wearing a bit thin with the participants, otherwise.

Such activities as factory visits and the interview exercise should be spaced out through phase one, rather than bunched at the end, in order to provide variety to the programme.

As in any short programme, it is essential to get things started on time, every session. Unless this is made a matter of pride with the participants, the leader will lose half the class at every session, because of people arriving late.

Good secretarial assistance and duplicating facilities are important for phases one and three of the workshop. Several exercises will only work well if the leader is able to have the participants' work typed and duplicated almost overnight.

If possible, the leader should have an administrative assistant available throughout the workshop, to conduct the inevitable negotiations concerning accommodation, arrange for transportation for factory visits and many other details that require someone who is not directly committed during the hours of the workshop sessions. The administrative assistant can do much advance work, as well, such as selecting and arranging for the venue.

It is appropriate for the workshop leader to remember that what is being taught is case method and case writing. The leader's teaching style should therefore be compatible with case method and the instructions to case method teachers contained in Chapter 5.

Finally, it is highly desirable for the workshop leader to be flexible and calm. It is comforting to remember a point that was made in an earlier chapter: case method teaching is very forgiving. A point that has been missed during the discussion of one case may well be picked up from a later one. This is true even of the points to be made in a short workshop programme. Some points can even wait to be made until phase three, if necessary.

Appendices 12 and 13 contain sample documentation related to workshop organisation: an invitation, instructions to accompany a timetable and a case evaluation form for use by participants. A list of cases and readings used in prior workshops is given in Appendix 14.

INSTITUTIONAL SUPPORT OF CASE METHOD

14

Chapter 12 suggested ways in which a single institution could introduce case method teaching in its own curriculum. Chapter 13 described case writers' workshops, the single most important activity required to build towards a "critical mass" of case writing ability in an institution, country or region. This chapter covers a number of other elements which are important for the regional spread of case method. Three of these elements are inter-related: an association of case writers, provision for publication of cases either as case books or in loose-leaf form, and the difficult issue of judging the merit of newly written cases. The last part of this chapter details some considerations of special relevance to cases and case writing in developing countries.

An association of case writers

Soon after the first class meetings of case writers' workshop, the participants are likely to raise the question, "why can't we form an association of case writers in our region?". One of the ways to achieve the above-mentioned "critical mass" of case writers in a region is to provide for continuing case writing activity by those who have learned to write cases. In the early days of case writing few persons at any one institution will have such experience. A way to foster continuing interest and activity is to form an association.

A number of regional associations of case writers grew up in the United States in the years following the workshops at Harvard. The continuing emphasis of these associations on introducing new writers to the techniques of case writing has been important not only in the spread of case writing but also in the growth of case teaching at many institutions. For several years the

Intercollegiate Case Clearing House (ICCH) aided these associations financially by partial support of an annual meeting at which new cases were discussed. Other expenses of the associations were covered by dues paid by members. Members of a typical association were required to show their continuing commitment by writing new cases each year for presentation at the annual meetings. One such association has case writing competitions each year. To be eligible for the competition, teams of two case writers, one an experienced association member and the other inexperienced, must submit two new field cases. These cases are read by anonymous referees. Writers of cases judged satisfactory by the referees are invited to the annual workshop, which is much like a large phase three workshop described in Chapter 13.

This short description of the association experience in the United States raises several questions which must be answered before giving unqualified endorsement to an association in a new context. While the association is small and struggling to survive, who will pay the expenses incurred in holding the meetings necessary to accomplish the association's purposes? How will the association provide not only for the preservation of interest in case writing among existing members, but also for fostering interest in others? What are the qualifications for membership? How will other bona fide case writers, who may not have attended a workshop, be recognised for membership?

A spontaneous association which merely plans to keep alive the acquaintanceships formed at a workshop should not be discouraged. It would, however, be a mistake to assume that such an association would accomplish broader goals. In order for a case writers' association to continue in existence and grow, it must have institutional support for a few years at least. Its initial membership should probably be 20 or more. An institution which planned to operate a case clearing-house or to publish case books would do well to plan ahead for sponsoring such an association.

Publication of cases –
case clearing-houses[1]

Even the most prolific case writers are unable to supply all the cases they need through their own efforts alone. Some means must exist for sharing cases among many authors. There are two principal institutional responses to this need: published case books and case

---

[1] See the list of case clearing-houses reproduced in Appendix 15.

clearing-houses for loose-leaf cases. In industrialised
countries, these functions are performed by different
institutions. Publishers generally sell case books
where markets are large enough to make them profitable.
Clearing-houses typically hope to break even on their
operations, at best.

Until markets for cases in developing countries
become large enough to attract publishers, it is probably
just as well to consider the field open to any institution that is willing to sponsor case method. The choice
between printing a case book or providing loose-leaf
cases can be made on the basis of relative costs and
benefits. It is likely that an institution must establish a case library if it hopes to gather enough cases
for either activity. Before undertaking publishing or
clearing-house activities, however, one should be sure
that no other nearby institution is performing this
costly function adequately for one's region. Clearing-
house activities are expensive to perform properly.
Fixed costs are relatively high, which means that there
should be few clearing-houses. A single clearing-house
has well served the needs of United States institutions,
which constitute the largest market for cases. Officials of the ICCH have been very helpful in giving advice
to new clearing-houses, and they can tell one at any time
where the other active case clearing-houses are, around
the world.

If it appears desirable for an institution to
establish its own clearing-house, the following are the
functions that must be performed, and the policy decisions that must be made.

Classification and numbering of cases. A scheme
such as that used by ICCH should be considered. ICCH
uses a seven-digit number, in which the first digit
identifies whether there are any restrictions on the
widespread issuance of the case (see later paragraphs
regarding release). The second digit identifies the
subect area, the third and fourth digits the year in
which the case was catalogued. However, earlier ICCH
cases are identified by volume numbers 01 through 14.
The last three digits are serial numbers which distinguish individual cases.[1]

Any new case clearing-house would want an alphabetical prefix attached to its case numbers, to identify

---

[1] See figure 5. For more details concerning
numbering refer to case bibliographies published by the
ICCH.

the source of the classification. Without this pre-
caution, as clearing-houses are set up at different
centres confusion will arise among cases with identical
numbers. From the beginning, one should adopt the
practice of printing the proper identification number at
a standard place on each page of every case.

Acceptance of cases and assurance of release.
Provision must be made for acceptance of cases. In the
beginning the problem may be one of persuading authors
of good cases to allow them to be issued through a new
clearing-house. Later on, an established clearing-house
may find itself deluged with case-like materials, for
which there may be little demand. This latter situation
is particularly likely where acceptance of a case by the
clearing-house becomes recognised as tantamount to
"publication". In the long run it may be necessary to
adopt a system of referees, as suggested in a later paragraph, in order truly to exert quality control over
cases in the clearing-house system. In the short run,
provision should be made to minimise the expenses associated with acceptance.

One good way to keep costs low is to require the
author of a new case to provide a reproducible original
and a specified number (perhaps 25) of copies of the
case. This reduces the cost associated with acceptance
and issuance of sample copies of the case to prospective
adopters. The author should also supply an information
sheet which includes an abstract of the case and whatever
other information the clearing-house plans to feature
in its bibliographies. The clearing-house needs only to
add its identification number, log the case in, and provide for storage.

A most critical element in acceptance is assurance
that the case has been released for widespread use.
The release procedure has been referred to in Chapter 10
as a protection for the case writer. It is equally
critical that a release be in order before a case is
duplicated and sent to teachers other than the writer.
The practical way for the clearing-house to proceed is to
require the author to sign a certification to the following effect.

I am the author of the case (case name), which is based on (cross out those which do not apply)

(a) field research;

(b) generalised experience;

(c) library or published source research.

   If based on field research, I cerfity that I have a release form signed by a responsible executive of the organisation involved, which authorises use and widespread distribution of the case.   If written from generalised experience or based on research in the library or published sources, I authorise use and widespread distribution.

Date _____   Signed _____

                          Title _____

                          Institution _____

   In the early days of case writing in a new environment workshop leaders, experienced case writers and clearing-house managers must foster in case writers the professional attitude that leads companies to accept further case writing.   The signed release form does little but record the fact of acceptance, but it is a critical component of the system, and the author's responsibility not to use field material without release must be emphasised.

   Storage and retrieval are easy in the beginning and become more difficult as numbers of cases on file grow. Metal filing cabinets with cases filed in numerical order in file folders or envelopes serve the purpose well in the beginning, and will serve continuously for active cases.   The reproducible original may be kept with the copies, although separately identified to prevent it being sent out as a copy.   To standardise storage and retrieval at least cost, certain decisions should be made early and then insisted upon:

- decide whether cases are to be on letter size, legal size or any other standard size sheet, and require incoming master copies of cases to conform;

- require new cases to be typed single space and with margins of adequate size to accommodate your planned system for binding;

- define what constitutes a "reproducible original" according to your duplication equipment and system;

- print cases on both sides of the sheet of paper.

   Duplication and issuance.   It is highly desirable
for a new clearing-house to charge enough for loose-leaf
cases to cover at least its variable costs.   (There may
be any number of good reasons, however, why a clearing-
house might prefer to ask for enough support money to
enable them to issue cases free until case method becomes
effectively established.)   The appropriate way to charge
is by the page.   Thus, someone who ordered 10 copies of
a 15-page case would pay 150 times the price per page.
If postage charges are likely to vary widely among
customers, it is useful to add actual or estimated actual
postage to the invoice.   Handling costs, for a small
clearing-house, are nearly a fixed cost, and may well be
absorbed by the sponsor who covers the other fixed costs.

   One of the most annoying problems for a case
clearing-house is to have its cases copied by someone else
without authorisation.   Particularly is this annoying
when a case is copied by retyping a new master copy;
usually this introduces many typographical errors, with
a consequent reduction in the teaching value of the case.
Furthermore, when a case has been revised by its author,
earlier versions being copied by other institutions can
lead to confusion.   The clearing-house should take four
steps to minimise the problems of duplication by others:

- It should keep its per page costs and charges for
  multiple copies as low as possible, so as to dis-
  courage others from copying to save money.

- It should offer to supply a reproducible master
  copy at a fair price so that a large and remote
  customer can legitimately make multiple copies to
  save time and shipping expense.

- It should carefully identify by adding to the title
  and number of any revised case the letter R.   For
  example, the original case might be "North Company",
  number 9-775-034.   The revised case would be "North
  Company (R)" 9-775-034R.   Subsequent revisions, if
  any, would be identified by subscripts, as "North
  Company (R2)", etc.

- It should point out in its promotional material the
  potential adverse effects of copying by any other
  means than photographic.

   Promotion of case use is an important function of a
clearing-house.   Teachers will need to be able to see
sample copies of cases, and their attention must be
attracted to a case in some way.   The preparation of a
comprehensive bibliography of cases available, giving

148

abstracts and other data similar to that offered in
ICCH's bibliographies (see Chapter 6), is an effective
method.   Eventually the clearing-house will need to
recover the costs of its bibliographies.   In the early
days, when mailing lists are small and the number of
entries in the bibliography limited, they should be sent
free as a way to promote interest in case method.

Another means of promoting the use of cases is for
the clearing-house to idenfity case "packages" to meet
special teaching objectives.   In the extreme this would
amount to choosing cases for an entire course.   Where a
clearing-house is attached to a university, it may ask a
professor's permission to issue lists of the cases used
in sequence in his/her course.   Some professors may be
reluctant to give this permission, for a number of legi-
timate reasons.   If the professor believes that cases
he/she has written can be made into a saleable case book,
or if some of the cases being used are being taught under
a "limited" release, or merely have not yet been taught
frequently enough for him/her to be sure they are ready
for widespread distribution, permission may not be
granted.   If a teacher is using primarily cases written
by others and available through the clearing-house, however, it should be possible to get co-operation in the
cause of promoting case method.

Promotion of case writing.   Usually the idea of
starting a clearing-house grows up after an institution
has sponsored workshops.   It is well to realise that the
clearing-house, once established, must continue to promote
case writing.   The mere fact of making cases widely
available is, in itself, a form of promotion, since it
promises authors an audience.   Beyond this, clearing-
houses will want to sponsor case writers' workshops to
the extent that groups of sufficient size can be brought
together.   Sponsoring a case writers' association
encourages new case writing efforts.   Whether the
clearing-house should proceed further, to establish relations with individual case writers as publishers often do
in the United States, is a matter of policy which must be
decided by the sponsors of the clearing-house.   This and
other policy matters are discussed in following paragraphs.

Major policy issues of clearing-houses

Three major policy issues face a new clearing-house;
decisions about these issues markedly affect all aspects
of the operation, including space needs, staffing and
budgets.   These issues are:

- What will be the clearing-house's primary service area?

- What will be the scope of its services?

- Will the clearing-house adopt a passive or an active role?

The <u>primary service area</u> issue involves choosing a large enough geographic market area to justify the expense to the sponsoring agency. Yet the area should not be so large as to result in poor response time to requests for cases. Increasingly, as clearing-houses are set up around the world, proposed clearing-houses are justified only if they can show that their primary service areas are not effectively served from an existing location. No hard and fast rules can be laid down concerning optimum geographic spacing. Probably no country needs more than one clearing-house, and several countries in a region who share a common language can often be served by a single centre. One house can act passively to make available cases in several different languages without excessive extra expense. To adopt an active role in developing cases in several languages, however, would be far more expensive.

The choice of <u>scope of services</u> is inter-related with service area. A clearing-house can view its services as largely supplemental to those of other centres. In such an instance, the new house would collect and issue regionally relevant cases, while urging its user-clients to rely on other centres for cases written earlier and in other regions. At the other extreme, a clearing-house might attempt to stock a broad enough selection of cases and notes, wherever written, to serve all the needs of case teachers in its service area.

The choice of broad or limited scope of service has obvious implications for inventory of cases. A new clearing-house would do well, the author believes, to choose a limited scope in the beginning, and to devote its resources and its management attention to the development of regionally relevant cases. An exception to this should be made, however, regarding cases from abroad which "fill out" the case course packets mentioned above as a promotional device. A management teacher may be more easily attracted to using cases if a coherent package is available from a single source.

The decision about scope of service is complicated by the fact that in the early days of any clearing-house it falls heir on one way or another to copies of a good many cases originally issued by other houses. Although perfectly sound techniques for keeping such things straight exist, and inter-house co-operation is easy to arrange for, it only takes one or two careless retypings of cases for all of the original indications of source to disappear.   In some instances, therefore, clearing-houses themselves perpetuate the problems mentioned in an earlier paragraph, of cases that have lost a good deal of their teaching integrity.

Sometimes these retypings come about as the result of an attempt to "regionalise" a case by changing the names and locations specified in the case and by changing monetary units from foreign to local ones.   The thought is that the case thus becomes more usable in the region. The author believes that such changes should not be made without co-ordination with the originator of the case. Except in the simplest of circumstances, the mere chang-ing of local currencies (e.g. Indian rupees) into their official exchange rate equivalents (e.g. US dollars) is more likely to mislead students about the underlying relationships than to clarify the case.   The students are likely to believe that relationships among the prices of consumer goods and the cost of a major piece of machinery in the United States should hold true in India. By contrast, the case in its original form convinces the students that they will have to re-examine all relation-ships before making decisions.   Apart from language translations, the author believes that only the original case writer should make changes in a case, for whatever reason.   Too many things can go wrong with the teaching quality of a case in the process of change.

The choice of an active or passive role for the clearing-house has a major impact on the size and charac-ter of the centre's staff.   A passive role involves offering services only to those who seek one out.   This is largely a library function, supported only by a cata-logue of materials available and the ability to retrieve them.   Earlier paragraphs have suggested that the author believes a new clearing-house must go beyond that role, at least to the extent of giving broad distribution to bibliographies, supporting case writing workshops and giving financial and administrative help to case writers' associations.   Maintaining a staff of people who travel throughout the service area to conduct workshops and develop contacts with individual case writers is an even more active stance.

Decisions regarding role can be made progressively. A clearing-house rarely arises except as a result of a somewhat active role by the sponsoring institution. If other institutions and a viable association come for-ward quickly, the clearing-house can perhaps afford to become more passive.   Otherwise it faces a choice between remaining moderately active or of undergoing the additional expense of more activity.

When a clearing-house chooses a highly active role, offering broad services to a wide geographic area, fixed costs of operation will be at their highest. Conversely, choosing a passive role, a restricted scope of services and a small service area minimises the fixed costs of the clearing-house.

Judging the merit of cases and of case writing activity

One continuing issue in the development of case method is whether writing cases is a "scholarly" activity, on a par with writing an article for publication in a refereed journal. In developing countries this issue will have to be faced by any institution which hopes to foster case method teaching, and particularly case writing. Unfortunately in this instance experience in developed countries offers little to go on.

The situation in the United States is this. Except at a handful of universities noted for their dedication to case method, case research and case writing are thought of in much the same way as are consulting and preparing lecture notes. "Publishing", to prevent "perishing", must be evidenced by articles appearing in "scholarly", by which is meant "refereed", journals. Despite much bewailing by case writers, cases do not "count" as publications. Some case writers believe that a good way to raise the status of case writing would be for the clearing-house (ICCH, in this instance) to set up a panel of referees and to accept new cases only when the referees judge them to be good ones. Other suggestions involve sponsorship by case writers' associations of subject-area "case journals", edited as are other scholarly journals. Only after decades of case writing in the United States are some steps being taken to referee cases. As yet only a small proportion of new cases are subject to being judged in this way, and it is still too early to know whether the new systems will have the desired effects.

Yet it is clearly appropriate that some means of quality control should be introduced, and equally important that the authors of good teaching cases based on research should be recognised and rewarded. Perhaps this is a role that should be played in new case development areas by sponsors of clearing-houses, either directly or through associations of case writers. It goes beyond the purpose of this manual to recommend anything but that

sponsors of case method be aware that such a policy
question must be decided.

It is the author's opinion that experienced case
teachers can judge whether a new case is a good teaching
vehicle.   Taken together with a comprehensive teaching
note, it is also possible to judge whether a case adds
substantially to our understanding of management pheno-
mena.   It would be entirely appropriate if two levels
of recognition and reward for case writing grew up.
The first level would be for the many good teaching cases
that are needed to bring well researched but fairly commonly occurring situations before students.   The second
and higher level would be for the relatively few cases
which, in addition to being good teaching vehicles, also
represent the bases for conceptual breakthroughs in the
field of management education and training.

Cases and case writing in developing countries

Throughout this publication there are frequent
references to developing countries, where case method
can make an exceptional contribution to more rapid
development of managerial competence without having to
transpose foreign concepts learned in a different context.   Yet it is in those very regions where the fewest
cases have as yet been written.

Several sorts of cases are especially needed in
developing countries:

- cases about entrepreneurship and new and small
  enterprises;

- production and operations management cases, with
  emphasis upon maximising productivity and efficiency;

- cases dealing with technological choice, because
  the appropriate mix of machines and manpower differs
  in each environment;

- cases dealing with the management of public enterprises in those countries where there is a large
  public sector involvement in industry and trade;

- cases dealing with international trade and/or
  multinational business relationships from the viewpoint of local interests, rather than from the
  viewpoint of the United States or Europe;

- cases about public policy and its impact on development; and

- cases written about the activities and circumstances of agencies, both local and international, whose purposes are to foster development and to implement important development projects or programmes.

If the opportunities for making an impact through cases are great, the difficulties facing case writers in developing countries are formidable, as well. Distrust of the motives of people who come around asking questions and taking notes is widespread among executives who are not at all sure of themselves. This distrust is greater in developing countries, where small numbers of firms in any given industry make disguise more difficult. With disguise difficult, the disclosure of "inside" information seems more potentially damaging. Lacking long experience with published annual reports containing detailed operating statements, many executives in developing countries cannot feel comfortable in disclosing such data to a researcher. Some may believe that if the cost and price relationships of the industry become known through cases that it may encourage new competitors to enter the field. In general, case writers in developing countries find it very difficult to gain access to financial and accounting data.

A second problem with case writing in developing countries is the absence of representative companies in some industries. It may be necessary to write a case about a company in a neighbouring country, in order to find an appropriate field site.

Other problems of case writing in developing countries stem from the lack of infra-structure, mainly communications and transportation. It is fair to point out that these same shortcomings frustrate managers in carrying out their own day-to-day tasks. Irregular postal services, unreliable telephone and telegraph and overcrowded transportation networks add both to the time and expense of writing cases. It becomes especially important to gather the information needed for a case by personal visits, and "call backs" for additional information are very time consuming. All in all, it is appropriate to plan for more time to discover and write a case in this context than in other parts of the world.

Last but not least, there is the well-known problem of an acute shortage of experienced management teachers and trainers who would be skilled not only in using case studies in the classroom but, in particular, in writing new and original local cases. Both as a very efficient way to teach them about case method and as a means of building up the stock of locally relevant cases, willing teachers should be exposed to case writers' workshops. As the new case materials begin to pile up, a means of widely disseminating the materials must be developed; a case clearing-house is one such means which has proved to be effective.

It will, of course, be essential to reward teachers for using and producing good quality cases. The rewards can be in terms of recognition, points towards promotion, release time to produce new cases and so forth. The critical issue is to assure that teachers and trainers who use the case method are not placed at a disadvantage compared to those who do not. Good quality cases can be counted as professional publications for promotional purposes both at university faculties and at the governmental or private management centres. The production of relevant case material should be valued as highly as consulting for business and government.

In short, the institution that seeks to sponsor the case method as one important tool in fostering management development must be ready to commit resources over a period of years and to struggle for necessary changes in regulations, traditions and work habits to:

- build a "critical mass" of teachers who know, understand and use the case method effectively;

- create an organisational climate in which the use and development of cases are seen as a highly respected and rewarding professional activity;

- see to it that cases based on local and regional conditions are written and properly released for use in the classroom; and

- provide for widespread dissemination of these cases, so that many institutions can afford to adopt the case method in their teaching and training.

APPENDICES

Case: Aluminium Sauce Pans, Ltd.

Abstract

The manager of a small-scale factory is concerned over how many additional machines he must buy to increase his production to meet demand.   The case provides raw material prices, sales prices of the completed products, a description of the production process, labour force, and production rate data.   The site is a developing country.

Possible teaching plan

This case could be taught on two levels.   On level one, for a very early case in operations management, the class could focus on two or three simple actions which could be taken to increase production without buying new machines.   The factory is on one-shift operation, for example.   A second shift would likely be a much better bet than buying new machines.   Furthermore, a total of two hours out of nine in the sample day are lost to production because the machines are idle while workers have lunch and their tea and coffee breaks.   In light of the fact that labour is plentiful and cheap, an increase of two-sevenths, or almost 30% could be achieved by providing additional workers to man the machines while other workers took their breaks.

At the second level, the case can be used to teach economic lot size calculations.   Many productive machine hours are being lost because the machines are down for

---

This case was written by John I. Reynolds and is intended for classroom use.   It is not intended to exemplify either effective or ineffective management. It can be used with Part I of this manual.

changing from one die size to another at too frequent intervals. A "first cut" would be to schedule die changes before or after the regular working day. Beyond that, however, it is possible to decide on a reasonably scientific basis how often the dies should be changed in order to achieve maximum output. At this second level, also, the class should focus upon the optimum scheduling of products in order to reach the desired mix of scales.

ALUMINIUM SAUCE PANS, LTD.

In July 1974 the production and operations management class of Professor Stephen Wamble visited a small-scale factory in the industrial district of Dangavia, capital of Tanganya, a developing country. As he showed them around the factory, the manager of Aluminium Sauce Pans, Ltd., explained that he needed to know how many additional stamping presses to buy. Despite his all-out efforts, production of saucepans seemed to fall continually behind demand, and the stamping operation seemed to be the "bottleneck", preventing an increase in output.

History

Aluminium Sauce Pans, Ltd., had been operated for a number of years past under private sector management. After it had fallen idle for several months in late 1973, the factory had been acquired by new owners who had little experience either in production or in sales. The manager therefore welcomed the visit of the class, saying he hoped the students could help him decide what steps to take to improve operations.

The product

The company made aluminium saucepans of varying depths and diameters, each with a rim about 2 cm wide. The pans were usually sold in nested sets of 3 to 7 sizes; each pan was designated by its diameter in centimetres. Exhibit 1 shows the product line of the company with selling prices currently in effect.

The production process

Each saucepan was formed in a single stroke of a stamping press. A stamping press was a machine about 3 m high, which could move a vertical piston through a stroke of about 70 cm, exerting many hundreds of

kilograms of force per cm^2 of area.   In order to determine which product would be made with each stroke, the
press was equipped with two halves of a die.   The bottom
half, which was hollow and formed the outside shape of
the pan, was mounted on the platform of the press.   The
upper half of the die, which was a solid cylinder and
formed the inside surface of the pan, was mounted on the
end of the piston of the press.

For each saucepan the press operator centred a
circular disc of aluminium of the proper diameter over
the hollow half of the die.   He then threw a switch
which caused the solid half of the die, mounted on the
piston, to force ("draw") the aluminium into shape.   As
the piston withdrew and stopped, the operator pulled the
formed saucepan from the press and set it aside.   The
aluminium discs were lightly lubricated before being set
in the press, to avoid sticking.

The formed pans were put through various deburring,
cleaning and buffing operations before being stored
temporarily until they were made up into sets and placed
in the warehouse.   "Not that we have very many pans in
storage", the manager said with regret.   "In fact, we
cannot keep up with demand.   We have hardly any complete
sets in inventory - just a few hundred 31 cm pans and
several dozens of some of the smaller sizes.   We always
seem to run especially short of 19 cm pans, however."
The manager pointed out, however, that in the case of
every process except that of stamping, he could increase
the throughput on short notice by assigning additional
workers;   none of the processes other than stamping
depended upon scarce machinery.

Equipment

The only output-limiting equipment in the factory
consisted of four huge stamping presses.   The manager
pointed out that presses 01, 02 and 03 were all of about
the same size, and smaller than press 04.   "The three
smaller presses are only able to draw pans up to 23 cm in
size", he said.   "These pans are all made from thin
aluminium discs.   Press 04 can handle any size pan we
make, but is particularly useful for the three largest
sizes, which use thick aluminium, and therefore require
more pressure."

Although the manager was unable to give an estimate
of the standard operating rate for the machines, he was
happy to supply the record of the previous Friday's production record (exhibit 2) and to allow the class to
observe the machines at work.   The records kept by four

students, each of whom observed a different press for 30 minutes, are summarised in exhibit 3.

Labour

The manager pointed out that he had no difficulty in hiring unskilled labourers for Sh.7 per day, the local going rate. Press operators on the smaller presses typically earned Sh.8 per day, and on press 04, Sh.9 per day, since these jobs were considered semi-skilled. Although only one man tended each press, the manager said that several other workers could operate the presses. They were assigned to the presses whenever a regular operator was absent. The company had no training programme. The major skill required in operating the presses was in properly centring the aluminium disc. This was largely a matter of seating a proper-sized disc within the area of the die bounded by a slight ridge. Discs were usually of exact size. When a disc was improperly centred the result was a lop-sided pan, which was usually scrapped. The manager said that he believed the normal scrap rate was 10%.

In addition to the four press operators, the normal workforce of the factory included 12-14 other workers, who performed all other production processes, moved raw materials and work in process from place to place, and manned the storeroom. The manager directed all the workers, treating the operator of press 04, his most experienced man, as a "lead" worker to oversee things when the manager was absent from the factory floor. Each press operator made his own set-up changes, at intervals of a few hours, as the manager tried to keep his stocks in balance in sets.

Marketing

The factory manager could only guess at the total size of the market for saucepans. "We have operated 'hand-to-mouth' for three months, since the new owners took over, trying to catch up with demand. We believe that the former owners produced a total of 15,000 sets in the last full year of operation. Apparently those sales consisted of about 11,000 of set 01; 3,000 of set 02; and 1,000 of set 03. Our demand still seems to run in about those proportions, but we suspect that sales might reach 20,000 sets annually if we could supply that many."

162

Raw materials

Because saucepans were considered a basic necessity of life, the company had been allowed to import as many aluminium discs as they could process. It was these imported discs that were being used at the time of the class visit to the factory. The manager said that locally made aluminium discs were available at substantially lower prices than the imported discs. The local supplier made his discs from reprocessed scrap aluminium (see exhibit 4 for raw material and scrap prices). The manager said that he did not like to use the local discs, however, because "scrap rates are around 50% for local aluminium, which tends to catch and tear in the presses, rather than drawing smoothly into the pan shape". The company continued to experiment with local aluminium from time to time, in case imports would suddenly be cut off.

Conclusion

As Professor Wamble and his class thanked the manager for his courtesy in showing them around, he repeated his earlier request. "It is clear to me that the stamping presses are a bottleneck which restricts our output. I have sales literature from manufacturers offering new or used presses for immediate delivery. I could buy additional small presses for about Sh.75,000, or large ones at Sh.150,000, both prices including delivery and set-up. Those are the used machines; new ones are higher. What should I do?"

Exhibit 1:   Product line in July 1974

Item   Factory selling price

Set 01 (5 items)   Sh. 53 per set
  (One each 15 cm, 17 cm,
   19 cm, 21 cm and 23 cm)

Set 02 (3 items)   Sh. 98 per set
  (One each 19 cm, 25 cm,
   and 37 cm)

Set 03 (7 items)   Sh.170 per set
  (One each 15 cm, 17 cm, 19 cm,
   23 cm, 25 cm, 31 cm and 37 cm)

Individual pans:
   15 cm   Sh. 7
   17 cm   Sh. 9
   19 cm   Sh.11
   21 cm   Sh.13
   23 cm   Sh.16
   25 cm   Sh.28
   31 cm   Sh.43
   37 cm   Sh.61

Exhibit 2:   Production for the previous Friday

Hours	Presses			
	01	02	03	04
8-10	400(15 cm)	360(17 cm)	320(19 cm)	160(25 cm)
10-10.30	---------------- Coffee break ------------------			
10.30-12.30	(set-up change)	360(17 cm)	320(19 cm)	(set-up change)
	---------------- Lunch hour ------------------			
1.30-3	200(21 cm)	(set-up change)	240(19 cm)	60(37 cm)
3-3.30	---------------- Tea break ------------------			
3.30-5	200(21 cm)	180(23 cm)	(set-up change)	60(37 cm)

Total daily production by size:

        15 cm - 400   23 cm - 180
        17 cm - 720   25 cm - 160
        19 cm - 880   31 cm -   0
        21 cm - 400   37 cm - 120

        Total all sizes - 2,860

Exhibit 3: Observations of presses in operation

Press and size	Production during six 5-minute intervals						Scrap
	1	2	3	4	5	6	
01 (21 cm)	13	12	17	2[*]	18	10	7 units
02 (23 cm)	10	9	11	12	8	10	5 units
03 (15 cm)	0[**]	0[**]	20	22	18	24	2 units
04 (37 cm)	3	2	0[***]	0[***]	4	4	3 units

Notes:

[*] Worker paused to smoke a cigarette.

[**] Press set-up still being changed.

[***] Press stopped for adjustment of die - worker noticed excessive damage rate.

Exhibit 4: Raw material prices, July 1974

Discs for	Imported	Local	Value as scrap
15 cm	Sh. 4.40	Sh. 2.50	Sh. 1.50
17 cm	5.70	3.25	1.95
19 cm	7.10	4.05	2.40
21 cm	8.60	4.90	2.95
23 cm	10.20	5.80	3.50
25 cm	18.40	10.50	6.30
31 cm	28.30	16.15	9.70
37 cm	40.30	23.00	13.80

Abstract

A manager in a developing country falls heir to the management of a 20-employee shop which has until recently been making silencers ("mufflers") for automobiles. After a quick trip through the workplace, during which he sees the layout, the machinery and the available raw material, he must plan a programme to get the shop operating profitably.

Possible teaching plan

This case can be used as an early case in general management; it encourages students to develop short and medium-range plans which encompass management, production, marketing and to a limited extent finance.

SILENCERS, LTD. (A)

In early 1973, the firm of Steel Products Assemblers Ltd., of Central City, Tangandya, acquired all the remaining assets of Silencers, Ltd. (SL), in default of payment of a debt by SL's former owners, who left the premises and equipment, but no records. Steel Products' general manager, Mr. John Kabalega, took over the additional assignment of getting SL back into operation. SL's premises were located in Kongoni, a minor city some

----

This case was written by John I. Reynolds as a basis for class discussion and not as an example either of effective or ineffective management. It can be used with Part I of this manual.

150 miles away from Central City.   The trip between the
two cities took about three hours by a series of major
metalled (paved) highways.

Mr. Kabalega immediately made a trip to Kongoni to
familiarise himself with the factory, its products and
its workforce.   He discovered that a force of about 20
workmen had been engaged in turning out automobile
silencers (called "mufflers" in American terms) and the
associated exhaust pipes virtually by hand.

SL's factory was located on the edge of the
industrial area of Kongoni, and consisted of an L-shaped
building of about 1,000 m^2 in total extent, with a
covered shed in close conjunction, where two cars at a
time could be driven up over open pits for servicing
them.   The entire frontage of the building, which
fronted on a paved road, was taken up by office space and
a storeroom, where finished stock could be stored on
sturdy wooden shelves.   The front wall of the building
was plate glass, but the lower panels of the glass had
been painted out to block the view from the street.

Equipment

One of the former workmen of SL showed Mr. Kabalega
through the factory, following roughly the flow of materials in constructing a silencer, and explaining the use
of the simple machines and jigs as he went along.   The
process started in one end of the "L", where SL's ready
stores of exhaust piping and sheet steel (the principal
raw materials) were kept.   Neither of these materials
was being manufactured in Tangandya, and Kabalega could
find no record of any more stock being on order.   Neither
did he know how much stock was on hand, although there
seemed to be a substantial stock, in terms of tonnage of
steel.

The major pieces of powered machinery were 3 motor-
driven radial saws for cutting off exhaust pipe, 3 bench-
mounted drill presses of up to 1/2 inch chuck capacity,
a metal-turning lathe, and an electric arc-welding
machine.   Hand or foot powered machines included a sheet
metal shear capable of making straight cuts in sheet
steel up to 1 1/2 m in width, and of the thickness needed
for silencers; 2 sets of 3 metal rollers, which operated
much like the clothes-wringers on pre-automatic washing
machines, which turned flat sheets of steel into tubes of
the proper diameter for silencer bodies; 3 gear-assisted
tube-bending jigs, which made possible duplicating any
exhaust-pipe bend in any of the sizes of exhaust pipe
needed; 2 hydraulic-assisted hand presses which were
used, with a variety of dies, for flaring tubes and/or

silencer end pieces; and assorted hammers, mallets, punches, anvils and other simple hand tools. An acety- lene welding outfit and a paint-sprayer completed the list of tools and machines Kabalega could see as he went round the factory.

At the rear of the shed he saw a substantial pile of what looked like scrap lumber, nailed together in hap- hazard fashion. The workman lifted up one of the con- structions, and pointed out how it just fitted the con- torted shape of an exhaust pipe from a particular model car. Although the wooden piece may have originally been labelled with the model and year of car for which it gave a pattern, John could not see the label; the unruly pile of forms was behind the area which had been used to spray paint the finished silencers, and the wooden forms were of a uniform black colour, which had obliterated any markings on them.

The man who showed John Kabalega around the factory guessed, in answer to John's question, that the factory had been turning out about 20 units (a silencer and its associated exhaust pipe section constituted a "unit") per day. Although some models were more in demand than others, apparently SL might be called upon to make any of about 200 different styles and sizes of silencers. Al- though proprietary designs of silencers often call for intricate interior designs and many different materials, the silencers made by SL differed from one another prin- cipally in exterior dimensions and shapes. For example, each silencer would be a cylindrical or oval exterior shape, with a pipe running through the centre. The central pipe was pierced at intervals to allow the expand- ing exhaust gases to be dissipated between the pipe and the walls of the silencer. The space between the pipe and the exterior walls was packed with glass wool, further to reduce the noise of the exhaust system.

Despite the simple nature of the silencers produced by SL, it was clear to Mr. Kabalega that the dimensions of the finished unit were critical. Its bends and angles must be exactly right so that it would fit pro- perly under the car as a replacement for the damaged unit. Exhaust piping itself came in about 15 different diameters, he learned.

Mr. Kabalega knew that the former owners of SL had sold through a network of automotive supply dealers and garages throughout Tangandya, although by far the largest sales had been to Central City based outlets. Until recent months, SL had faced considerable competition from imported silencers, which the new car dealers (and their associated service organisation) preferred, despite their higher cost, to SL's products. As imports had slowed

down, SL's opportunities had increased.   In early 1973
it seemed likely that imports would be further curtailed,
perhaps eliminated, as had been the case with new
vehicles themselves.

Although very recent figures on vehicle registra-
tions were unavailable, Mr. Kabalega knew that there were
about 35,000 passenger cars and 5,000 lorries and buses
in Tangandya.   SL was not equipped to manufacture
silencers large enough for lorries and buses.

The former owners had been three brothers, who had
generally divided management responsibilities among themselves.   No significant records had been left concerning
the business, and no remaining employee had held a position higher than "lead worker".   All decisions on
scheduling or other management actions had been taken by
the owners themselves.   The former workers were generally
available for employment.

Mr. Kabalega was interested in setting down in an
orderly fashion some steps which he might take to get SL
into profitable operation.

If you were Mr. Kabalega what would you do?   How
would you go about it?   Why?

Abstract

In 1974 a new managing director of a parastatal (government-run) company must establish quickly the management information system he will need to grasp control of the business. The firm has consistently lost money in recent years. The only records he has to work from are intake and output records in physical units by month for 1973 and financial statements for 1971. He has a fairly complete description of the slaughtering process and an understanding of the mission assigned to the company by the Government.

Possible teaching plan

The case allows for the development of a blueprint for a management information system. The questions at the end of the case direct discussion to that purpose.

KENGANZIA BEEF, LTD.

In early 1974, Mr. Jacob Njoroge had just been appointed managing director of Kenganzia Beef, Ltd., a parastatal firm located in the industrial area of Capital City. He was distressed to discover that very few records or summaries of information had been kept by his predecessor in office, who had been dismissed by the Ministry of Industry because Kenganzia Beef (KBL) had been suffering losses for several years. Njoroge was a

---

This case was written by John I. Reynolds. It can be used with Part II of this manual.

man of considerable managerial experience, and he knew the importance, to a managing director, of information about the business, of the right types and the right quantities.

He knew, from the Act which had created KBL, that the firm's purpose had been to purchase beef cattle from farmers, slaughter the animals, and dress out the carcasses for sale through meat stalls and supermarkets in Capital City. In the early days of KBL (which had been started in the mid-1960s), there had been a surplus of cattle being offered for slaughter, in relation to local demand for beef. As a result, KBL had installed a freezer, and had developed a small export trade in frozen beef, facilitated by the fact that Capital City was on a navigable river with an outlet to the sea. This made it comparatively easy to load ships for beef-consuming nations.

Further, he knew that the Act called for KBL to "pay as high a price as possible to the farmer, while maintaining as low a price as feasible for beef sold to the local market, and, taking one year with another, earn such returns as would not require continuing government subsidies". Except for one or two years in the late 1960s, when the export trade had reached its height, KBL had required subsidies to make up deficits; it was this fact which finally led to Njoroge's appointment to replace the previous managing director.

He soon found out, by making a tour of the various premises of the firm, the following facts:

The firm maintained small stockyards, where up to 400 live cattle could be kept and fed prior to slaughter. Farmers brought cattle in truckloads to a weighing station at the entrance to these yards, where the total weight of cattle was determined by weighing the truck before offloading the cattle, and then immediately afterwards weighing the empty truck. As each truckload of cattle was held separately for a few minutes in an enclosure, an inspector examined the animals to determine the grade of meat which might be expected. KBL accepted all live and healthy animals which were brought in, but paid less for animals which because of age or condition were likely to produce lower quality meats.

KBL's slaughterhouse could process 100 animals per day. An animal was killed, skinned, and separated into "sides" which provided the primary products of KBL, fresh beef plus the saleable organs such as liver, heart, etc. Major by-products were the hides, which were sold "green" to tanners who came to the factory to remove them regularly, and a few other parts which could be made into

172

glue or fertiliser, which were also sold off to other firms.

Fresh beef was hung in refrigerated chambers, which had a holding capacity of 500 whole carcasses (1,000 sides) for at least two to three days, after which they were considered ready for sale.

Just adjacent to the factory, KBL had freezers which would quick-freeze 25 carcasses (50 sides) per day, and store up to 500 carcasses (1,000 sides). Frozen beef could be stored for months without deteriorating in quality, although the cost of storage was an important factor to consider.

KBL sold to the local (Capital City) markets through a number of wholesaler dealers, each of whom accepted delivery at the KBL factory. Wholesaler dealers ordered their beef on either of two bases:

(1) on long-term contract, for a total amount of beef per year, with orders for actual delivery placed two weeks in advance;

(2) on a "spot" basis, which meant that a wholesaler dealer might call in the morning to determine if beef was available, and send his truck to pick up his order.

Prices for local delivery were set by the Government and tended not to vary much from year to year.

The procedure for export selling was quite a bit more complicated, and the prices were much more variable. Generally, KBL received requests for quotations from brokers in foreign countries, which might call for shipments six months in the future, in lots of at least 250 sides per shipment. KBL realised prices for such shipments which were about 20% higher than the local prices for fresh, unfrozen beef, but it did not receive payment until after the beef had arrived at its destination, whereas in the case of local sales payment terms called for cash (for spot sales) or at the end of each month (for sales made against yearly contracts).

Beef for sale in the local markets was generally classified as "highest quality" (grade A), "medium quality" (grade B) or "low quality (grade C). Prices received for the three grades varied in the ratio of 100 (for grade A), 90 (for grade B) and 75 (for grade C). Rarely was KBL able to sell any quality except grade A in the export market.

KBL had 200 employees, of whom about 180 worked in and around the stockyards, slaughterhouse and factory. The remaining 20 were employed in the headquarters offices, in sales, accounts, personnel and administrative positions. Casual labour was easily available at the factory site for any extra work of handling and carrying, but the work inside the factory (slaughtering, skinning, and butchering) was either skilled or semi-skilled, and could not easily be supplemented by casual labour.

Among the few records which Mr. Njoroge could find were audited accounts for the fiscal year ended 2 1/2 years previous to his taking office, and monthly summaries of cattle accepted at the stockyards, sales to the local wholesale dealers, and export shipments.*

He was interested in setting up a set of simple reports for his own use, in getting control over both the effectiveness of the KBL operations and of the efficiency with which those operations were being carried out.

He also had received requests from subordinates:

(1)   extension of stockyards to a capacity of 600 live animals;

(2)   expansion of refrigerated storage for fresh beef, to 1,500 whole carcasses (3,000 sides).

Questions

1.   What major items of information does Mr. Njoroge need immediately, to round out his initial understanding of this business?

2.   What are the major measures of "effectiveness" for this business?

3.   What are some of the major measures of "efficiency" for this business?

4.   What reports should he ask for on a regular routine basis?

----

* Summarising these monthly statements quickly for the last year, Njoroge discovered that 16,000 animals had been accepted at the stockyards, 30,763 sides had been sold locally, and 750 sides had been exported (in just 3 export shipments, each of 250 sides).

174

Exhibit 1: Operating statement of KBL for 1971

		Shillings
Revenues		16 400 000
Costs of production:		
Cost of cattle	14 400 000	
Cattle feed	200 000	
Factory labour	240 000	
Power	440 000	
Depreciation	260 000	
Maintenance	160 000	
Supplies and spares	280 000	15 980 000
Operating profit		420 000
General and administrative expenses:		
Salaries of officers and staff	250 000	
Other administrative expenses	300 000	
Sales expenses	50 000	
Interest expenses	170 000	770 000
Net loss		350 000

Exhibit 2: Balance sheet of KBL for 31 December 1971

Shillings

Assets:

Current assets

Cash	1 500	
Debtors	1 900 000	
Stocks	300 000	
Total current assets		2 201 500

Fixed assets

Land		400 000	
Buildings	2 000 000		
Less accumulative depreciation	600 000	1 400 000	
Plant and equipment	1 600 000		
Less accumulative depreciation	960 000	640 000	
Total net fixed assets			2 440 000
Total assets			4 641 500

Equities:

Current liabilities

Creditors	1 250 000	
Bank overdraft	326 500	
Total current liabilities		1 576 500
Long-term loan from Government		1 460 000
Shareholders' equities – 40 000 shares at Sh.100	4 000 000	
Less accumulative losses	2 395 000	1 605 000
Total equities		4 641 500

Exhibit 3:   Summary of KBL activity reports for 1973

	Live cattle accepted	Sales (sides)	
		Local	Export
January	789	1 538	
February	911	1 585	250
March	1 042	1 905	
April	1 898	4 232	
May	1 154	2 148	
June	1 815	2 836	
July	1 238	2 450	
August	1 142	2 320	250
September	1 115	2 430	
October	1 165	2 338	
November	1 198	2 500	
December	2 542	4 484	250
Total	16 000	30 763	750

UHURU CANDLE COMPANY, LTD.

Mr. Joseph Ziggundu, who had recently joined the
Kengolia Industrial Development Board (KIDB) as a management trainee, received his first operating assignment in
the following terms. His immediate superior, Mr. John
Traino, called him into the office one morning and said,
"Joseph, you know that we have recently been told to take
over and operate a number of businesses which have previously been in private hands. One of these is the
Uhuru Candle Company (UCC), on Industrial Road about
6 km from Capital City. You know the area; there are
several car repair shops out that way, and on the same
plot as the candle company are a vegetable oil mill and
a maize mill. I want you to go out as soon as possible
and get the candle factory going again. George K. and
Frank W. are assigned to the two mills. Although the
owner's family operated the three businesses together,
there is no reason why that should be so now. The three
buildings share an entry drive and turnaround area, but
you shouldn't be too crowded under present conditions.
Just stay on friendly terms with George and Frank and
everything will be all right."

This case was prepared by John I. Reynolds and
Larry Gene Pointer of Texas A and M University. It is
designed to be used as a basis for class discussion
rather than to illustrate either effective or ineffective
handling of an administrative situation.

Presented at a case workshop and distributed by the
Intercollegiate Case Clearing House, Soldiers Field,
Boston, Mass. 02163. All rights reserved to the contributors. This case can be used with Part II of the
manual.

Joseph asked, "what information do we have about the candle company - its production or sales volumes, profitability, raw material needs, sales outlets - that sort of thing?".

"As you know, the circumstances under which this business and many others came to be our responsibility were such that we have no records, unless you find some out there. We don't even have keys. If you need to do so, break any locks and replace them with new ones you can draw from central stores.

"What is my operating budget?"

"We are hoping that there will be enough raw materials and supplies on hand for you to get started. There are no other candle makers in the country, and the demand has always been brisk. Once you get started, you will probably be able to keep going out of self-generated funds. We have not accepted liability for any debts of the previous owners, not even for wages which might be due to workers, so you do not need to concern yourself with funds until wages are due at the end of the first month or you need raw materials, whichever comes first. Your own salary will continue to be paid by KIDB as it has been during your training. It will appear eventually as a book-keeping charge against UCC. If you need any cash account at all, it will need fairly detailed justification; since our total KIDB budget was established long before we were saddled with all these extra businesses, we have no excess funds after getting some of the larger businesses off the ground."

As Joseph thanked his boss for the opportunity and turned to leave, Traino said, "I'm sure you will do just fine. It is my impression that management can be summed up pretty much in this way: a manager is a man who comes in in the morning and says 'all right, chaps, get on with it'. As soon as you have UCC running smoothly we'll find a couple of other businesses for you to watch over. We have about six businesses per manager on our plate right now."

Joseph Ziggundu drove to the UCC premises, where he asked the first person he saw, "which building is the candle factory?". The factory proved to be a converted bungalow (see floor plan, exhibit 1) nestled against one outer wall of the compound. He was somewhat relieved to find that he did not immediately need to break a lock to enter the house to look around. But he was at a bit of a loss to figure out just how to take the next step.

Luckily, the man who had directed him to the factory had added the gratuitous information that,

"Mary Y. used to work there, for a long time. She knows all about it". As Joseph wandered from room to room, he became aware of a woman who seemed to be hanging around, just outside the circle of his direct gaze. She did not avoid his confrontation when he turned to look at her, finally. She proved to be Mary Y., who had not found other employment after the UCC had closed, and apparently returned every day in hopes that something would turn up.

From Mary, Joseph learned how the production process worked, and also that a group of about 15 women had constituted the labour force. She pointed out a room where "the boss used to sit". That door hung ajar, its lock having previously been broken by some volunteer. A glance at the office furnishings convinced Joseph that he would not find useful records there. Apart from scraps and shreds of paper on the floor, the files and drawers had been cleaned out. The room Mary pointed out as the "storeroom" had fared better; its lock was intact. It later proved as Traino had hoped, the sufficient raw materials were on hand to begin operations. This Ziggundu started to do, believing that the quickest way he could learn the business of managing a candle factory was to get it going and observe the process. Most of the previous employees soon showed up when Mary Y. put the word around that UCC was open again, and Joseph had an opportunity to experience what it was like to say, "all right, get on with it". The former owners of the UCC and others of their countrymen had a reputation for being good businessmen, and Joseph reasoned that the methods and processes they had established would be worth his study and understanding.

The production process

The production process started with the twisting of single threads of cotton into a multiple-strand candle wick, which was done by two women in the area shown as "A" in exhibit 1. Mary Y. explained that the factory had originally imported the wick already twisted together and that the boss had seemed to prefer the imported wick, which she believed had cost Sh.3 (three shillings) per kilogram (kg). In the last few months of operation, however, the factory had been winding its own wicks form thread produced by a local cotton spinning mill. The process was a simple one, and the two women could keep up with the need for wicks except for rainy days, when a leak in the roof over area A made it difficult to keep the thread dry. Mary pointed out that when the wicks were wet they failed to take up the proper amount of candle wax.

The next step in the process was to wind the wick on one half of an iron frame which, when married with the other half frame, made up a mould into which 12 candles could be poured (see exhibit 2). Mary explained that the boss had been particularly strict about the frames. "Those frames cost Sh.300 each, more than 20 years ago", he would say, "today I don't know whether we could replace them at any price. Be careful." Joseph found 48 complete frames, each of which weighed about 5 kg.

When the wicking had been strung in the frames, and the two halves of each frame joined together by two women working at a bench in area B, one or two women carried the frames into the filling room, area C. There they set the frames upright, end-to-end on benches along the walls or in the centre of the room. In area C two women with tea kettles filled with hot paraffin walked from frame to frame, pouring them just to overflowing; it took two passes, the second after a short interval for the first wax to settle, to assure that each candle would be complete and round. A tea kettle filled with wax weighed about 3 kg.

The two wax pourers drew their tea kettles of wax from spigots near the bottoms of two drums of hot wax in the next room (area D). These drums were heated by burners fueled with bottled gas. Mary Y. explained, and Joseph observed, that she was responsible for lighting the gas burners at 8 a.m. when the women reported to work. When the drums contained all new blocks of paraffin, it seemed to take about 2 1/2 hours for the wax to reach the right consistency for candles. When it was just a matter of reheating wax left over from the day before, perhaps with just a block or two of new wax, pouring could begin after 1 1/2 hours.

After the filled moulds had set for a few minutes - Mary said it took about 20 minutes after the last wax had settled, and this seemed to Joseph to be about right - women carried the frames to area E, where two women opened them and lifted the candles out, to harden for a few more minutes in the air on benches in that area. Next a group of women "finished" and packed the candles. Finishing consisted of cutting off or smoothing any unsightly mould marks, trimming flat the candle bottoms and cutting the wicks to the proper length. During this process any broken or imperfectly moulded candles were rejected and set aside for remelting and reuse of the paraffin. Mary Y. told Joseph that, "when everything is going well, the wicks are dry and the wax is at the right temperature, we almost never have any damaged candles". During the first few days of operations Joseph observed that such damage seemed to average about 300 candles per day, with the heaviest incidence of damage during the

first pouring round when, he judged, the women were
anxious to get started, some times before the wax was hot
enough.

After finishing, candles were packed in area F.
First the packers placed 6 candles in a thin cardboard
box; then they packed 12 boxes in a corrugated carton.
Then they stacked the cartons in area G ready for sale.

Joseph soon found that Mr. Traino was right about
demand for candles. Hardly had he opened the factory on
the first day before would-be customers were driving up
in trucks, jeeps, private cars and even on bicylces to
buy at the factory door. Although Joseph was too busy
to spend time comparison shopping, he heard from his wife
that candles were still so scarce that they were often
offered in Capital City shops at Sh.10 for a box, as
against the suggested retail price of 75 cents (100 cents
= 1 Shilling) per candle. Two of his fellow KIDB
manager-trainees, who had received assignments at up-
country locations, wrote to ask him why his candles were
never displayed for sale up country. They said that the
only available candles in their locations were those
smuggled in from neighbouring countries, and that a
typical price was Sh.3 or more per candle. In any
event, Joseph usually had little trouble selling all his
daily production before noon of the following day, for
cash at the price of Sh.32.40 per carton of 72 candles,
which was the allowed factory sales price under Kengolia
government rules.

The product and its ingredients

UCC's product was a white candle about 25 cm long
and 2 cm in diameter, which weighed about 45 grams. The
candle "wax" was paraffin, which UCC bought from a local
affiliate of an international petroleum company for
Sh.5.60 per kg. The paraffin came in blocks weighing
10 kg each, packed four blocks to a plastic bag package,
which was itself over-wrapped with gunny sacking.

The cotton threads for wicks came from a local
cotton spinning mill, and the most recent purchase made
by the former owners had been at 50 cents per kg. Both
the thin cardboard boxes and the corrugated cartons had
been imported, apparently at a cost of 15 cents per box
and 60 cents per carton. Joseph found that he had about
50,000 boxes and 4,000 cartons on hand. He made a note
to check about potential local suppliers for these items,
since he believed it would be difficult to get foreign
exchange entitlements for paper supplies. The local
sales representative of the petroleum firm told him not
to worry about continuing availability of paraffin or

bottled gas.   His firm had supplied fuel to Kengolia's
armed forces for several years, and he had been assured
of ample foreign exchange to import any and all petroleum
products.   Although Joseph saw that he started with 80
sacks of paraffin on hand, he was happy to know that
supplies could be replenished, albeit for cash, when
needed.

The results of the first few days

Joseph was pleasantly surprised at the bustle of
activity which resulted after he told Mary Y. to "get on
with it".   He had told the 15 women that they would be
paid Sh.7 per day, a fairly standard wage for unskilled
labour in Capital City, and that they must be at the
factory promptly at 8 a.m. and not leave before 4 p.m.
Although the women tended to become somewhat specialised,
nearly all could do any job if someone was late or
absent, which happened often.   Only Mary Y. was allowed
to light the gas burners, however, and the jobs of carrying empty frames into the pouring room and bringing out
the sometimes hot full frames were relegated to the
less-experienced and younger women.   One job which
Joseph asked Mary about rarely seemed to get done.   That
was scraping up the wax which spilled on the benches and
the floor.   She explained the matter in the following
terms.

"One time, several years ago, the boss experimented
with coloured candles.   By adding some colour in the
mix, we could scrape up and remelt almost all the wax
from the benches and the floor.   The colour would hide
the dirt.   However, the coloured candles could only be
sold at a lower price (Joseph recognised the figure she
gave as about 10% below the previous price of white
candles), and yet they cost more, since the cost of the
colour was extra.   So the boss quit making coloured
candles, and we only scrape off and reuse the wax which
sticks to the moulds, or occasionally some very clean wax
from the benches.   The rest of the spills we get busy
and clean up when it gets dangerous and slippery."

From the first day's operations, Joseph had kept
records.   He could only estimate how much paraffin had
been caked in the two drums on the first day, and how
much gas remained in the two gas cylinders which had been
hooked up when he arrived.   He found out quickly that it
took only about two days to empty a full gas cylinder in
normal operation, and that refills cost Sh.55 each from
his friendly petroleum supplier.   Exhibit 3 shows a
sample of the records Joseph wrote down as they occurred.

Although it seemed to him that the women worked steadily, and at as fast a pace as was safe, considering the bustle of movement back and forth through the doorway of the pouring room, one afternoon he was surprised to have Mary tell him, "our old boss used to insist that we must get 11 'turns' (full cycles of filling and emptying the 48 candle moulds) per day, but we finally convinced him that 10 turns was all he could reasonably expect. Don't you think that is enough?" All Joseph could think of to say at the time was, "You all seem to be working very hard, considering the conditions."

Planning for the future

Joseph recognised that while UCC was working through its starting inventory of raw materials he was building up cash from sales, and that he would have no difficulty in meeting his first payroll at the end of the month, or even of buying new stocks of paraffin. He was anxious, however, to determine what his profits would be, since he would eventually be evaluated on how well he managed this business. He realised that a normal operation would have to pay his own salary of Sh.1,600 per month, as well as some overheads such as rent, insurance, electricity, telephone and the like, all of which were somewhat in abeyance for the moment. He wondered whether he should plan some capital expenditures, and whether the idea of depreciation on capital assets, even though they had not been paid for by his Government, might have some relevance in determining whether he was running a profitable business.

Finally, he wondered how he should take into account the underlying requirement, which he knew ran through all KIDB operations, that businesses should serve all the people of Kengolia. As the manager of the only candle factory in the country, did he have any special responsibility to assure even distribution throughout the land?

Exhibit 1 Floor plan of factory

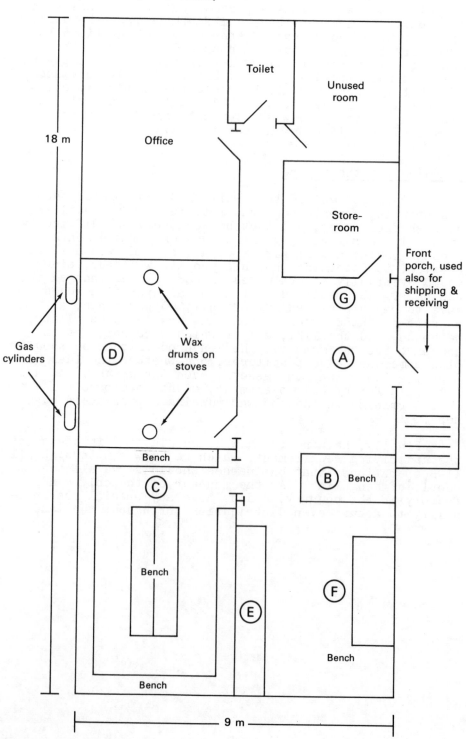

Exhibit 2   Candle mold frame

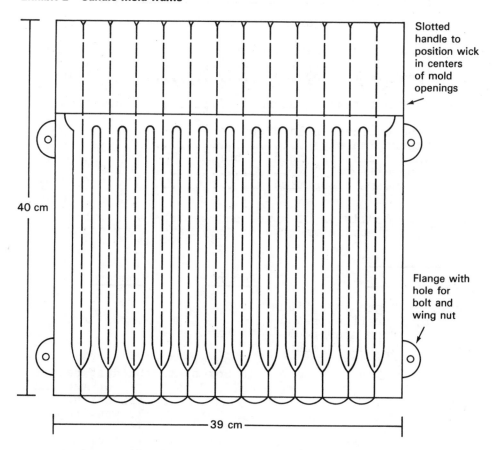

Part 1 of frame is shown above, as if open and strung with wick (wicking shown as dotted line). Part 2 of frame matches part 1 minus the handle section, and is secured to part 1 by four bolts and wing nuts.
Parts 1 and 2 when joined together are about 8 cm thick.

Exhibit 3: Sample of Joseph Ziggundu's records

Beginning inventory of raw materials and supplies:

- Paraffin hardened in drums
  (estimated) .... 150 kg
- Paraffin in storeroom .... 80 bags
  (40 kg each)
- Cotton thread in storeroom .... 200 spools
  (1 kg each)
- Candle boxes (hold 6 candles)
  (approximately) 50 000
- Candle cartons (hold 12 boxes)
  (approximately) 4 000
- Cylinders of bottled gas ....   2 (partly
                                             used)

Comment: Condition of boxes and cartons on bottom of
          stack is uncertain; may have water damage.

Daily records:

Date	Item	Amount	Comment
Mon., 16 Oct.	Began operations Paraffin issued from storeroom	4 bags	
	Cotton thread issued	6 spools	
	Sales	16 boxes at Sh.4.50 each	Sold at retail to workmen and friends of Mary Y. who dropped in.
	Cartons of finished candles at 4 p.m.	19 cartons	Most of last "turn" from moulds, several hundred candles, on benches awaiting finishing and packing.
Tues., 17 Oct.	Paraffin issued	6 bags	
	Thread issued	9 spools	
	Sales	19 cartons at Sh.32.40	Customers started coming at 10 a.m. Sold cartons finished yesterday.
		12 boxes at Sh.4.50	Perhaps should cease retail sales - dishonesty and confusion?

Date	Item	Amount	Comment
Tues., 17 Oct. (cont.)	Purchased 1 gas cylinder to replace one which went empty at 1 p.m.	Sh.55 paid	
	Cartons of finished candles at 4 p.m.	37 cartons	
Wed., 18 Oct.	Paraffin issued	7 bags	
	Thread issued	8 spools	
	Sales	40 cartons	Refused many retail sales requests.
	Purchases: 1 gas	Sh.55 paid	
	Cartons of finished candles at 4 p.m.	45 cartons	
Thurs., 19 Oct.	Paraffin issued	4 bags	Rained three hours; curtailed operations and discouraged sales.
	Thread issued	2 spools	
	Sales	28 cartons	
	Cartons of finished candles at 4 p.m.	60 cartons	
Fri., 20 Oct.	Paraffin issued	7 bags	
	Thread issued	9 spools	
	Sales	75 cartons	
	Purchases: 1 gas	Sh.55 paid	
	Cartons of finished candles at 4 p.m.	46 cartons	

Sat., (Decided to take physical inventory again.)
21 Oct.
(a.m.)

- Paraffin hardened in drums
  (estimate) .... 180 kg
- Paraffin in storeroom .... 52 bags
- Thread in storeroom .... 164 spools
- Boxes (approximately) 47 000
- Cartons (approximately) 3 800
- Candles awaiting finishing and
  packing 743

(Supplement)

During the two or three weeks following the events described in the case, Joseph Ziggundu continued to observe the operations, without making any changes in procedures or work assignments. Daily production continued at about the level of the first week, and he was always able to sell everything within a day or two of production. The following tables summarise his notes concerning his observations.

Table A: Results of 10 samples of candles poured and set under various conditions

Sample No.	Interval between pass 1 and pass 2	Set time after pass 2	Condition, comment
1	30 seconds	20 mins.	Reject - bottom not filled out
2	60 "	20 "	OK
3	90 "	17 "	Reject - too soft
4	120 "	15 "	Reject - too soft
5	150 "	20 "	OK
6	180 "	40 "	OK
7	240 "	19 "	OK
8	360 "	25 "	OK
9	480 "	30 "	Reject - separated at joint of passes
10	90 "	overnight	Reject - damaged in removing from frame

Special observations concerning wax:

(1) Wax should be poured from the kettle within 5 min. of drawing from the drum; otherwise it tends to set up and clog the kettle spout.

(2) A fairly complete clean-up of the paraffin spilled on benches and floors during a week takes three women, scraping with hoes, about 1 hours.

(3) The average weight of wax per candle, poured during the first pass, is about 35 grams. The average weight poured during the second pass, including the

extra wax which must be cut off in the finishing operation, in order to ensure a flat bottom, is 20 grams.

(4) Ten "kettlefuls" of wax, taken at random, averaged 2.9 kg in weight. The range was from 2.7 to 3.0 kg.

Table B: Results of two sample observations of location and condition of frames, activities of workers

Location	Condition or activity	Frames (No.) Sample 1	Sample 2	Workers (No.) Sample 1	Sample 2
A	Wick preparation			2	2
B	Empty, awaiting stringing	2	2		
B	Stringing, bolting	1	2	1	2
B	Strung, waiting	1	-		
B-C	Moving frames	2	2	1	1
C	Empty, waiting	14	10		
C	Pouring, first pass	1	2	1	2
C	Part-filled, waiting	6	7		
C	Pouring, second pass	1	-	1	-
C	Filled, "setting up"	14	16		
C-E	Moving frames	-	2	-	1
E	Filled, waiting	4	2		
E	Opening	1	1	1	1
E	Finishing candles			3	3
E	Frames open, waiting	1	-		
E-B	Moving frames	-	2	-	1
F	Packing candles			2	2
	Workers on "personal time"			2	-
	Workers absent			1	-
		48	48	15	15

Table C: Results of 10 observations of individual
          production operations

Operation	Times (seconds)		
	Minimum	Maximum	Average
Wick preparation (2 women per operation)			
1. Cut 4 strings 6 m long	20	40	30
2. Lay strands together, loose twist	30	50	40
Activities involving **frames**			
3. String 1 frame	50	90	60
4. Bolt 1 frame	30	80	60
5. Carry 2 frames B-C (1 woman)	15	50	30
6. Pour 1 frame, first pass	20	50	35
7. Pour 1 frame, second pass	15	40	25
8. Carry 2 frames, C-E (1 woman)	20	60	40
9. Open 1 frame	20	40	30
10. Lift out candles, 1 frame	15	60	30
11. Carry 2 frames E-B (1 woman)	15	30	20
Total of activities involving frames	200	500	330
12. Draw paraffin (1 round trip from C to D to C)	120	300	180
13. Inspect and trim 1 candle	5	30	15
14. Fold 1 box	8	15	10
15. Insert 6 candles, close box	10	22	15
16. Fold carton	12	30	20
17. Insert 12 boxes, close carton	25	40	30
18. Carry 3 cartons F-G (1 woman)	20	40	30

UHURU CANDLE COMPANY, LTD.

Teaching notes

I. Overview

A management trainee in an African development corporation receives his first operating assignment, to restart a candle factory which the Government has taken over from private owners. With experienced but unskilled labour he gets the factory going. Without previous records he must appraise performance and plan for the future. Major areas of concern are manufacturing layout, processes and controls; cash flows and profitability analysis.

II. Methodology

A floor plan and description of the production process allows for appraisal of the layout and flow of work, without need for any sophisticated techniques.

Sufficient information is given to allow for several approaches to profitability, including pro forma operating statements related to either expected yield from raw materials and labour or actual yield.

It is possible to construct a simple cash flow statement.

The ideas of fixed and variable costs, relevant costs and contribution each have a part to play in the analysis.

In the production area, the ideas of a "bottleneck operation", work sampling, simple time study, assignment of tasks and sequencing of operations all are pertinent.

III. Analysis

Questions to direct study analysis and class discussion:

(1) Can UCC be profitable, given present cost levels and government-controlled selling prices?

(2) Based on the first five days of operations, how well is UCC doing, financially?

(3) Should UCC produce coloured candles? If so, how
     would you determine the price to charge for them?

(4) What additional information does Joseph need, in
     order to determine a production target for the
     factory, given present equipment and processes?
     How would you use the additional information?

(5) Should Joseph make any changes in factory layout
     and/or production processes? If so, what would you
     suggest and why?

There are several ways in which students might approach
the case.   The following analyses would be useful in
answering the above questions in the order given.

Question 1

Table 1: Pro forma daily partial operating statement
          (assuming 10 "turns" and salvage of damaged
          candles)

Output (10 turns x 48 frames x 12)   5 760 candles
     Less: estimated damaged candles   300
                                                       -----
                                                     5 460

Value of saleable output $\frac{5\ 460}{72}$ x Sh.32.40   Sh.2 457

Raw materials costs:

Wax (5 460 x 0.045 x Sh.5.60)	1 376	
Thread (assume 6 at Sh.0.50)	3	
Boxes ($\frac{5\ 460}{6}$ x Sh.0.15)	136.50	
Cartons ($\frac{5\ 460}{72}$ x Sh.0.60)	45.50	1 561
		896

Operating costs:

Gas (Sh.55 x 0.5)	27.50	
Labour (15 x Sh.7)	105	132.50

Contribution towards profit and
unidentified costs: 763.50
                                                            ======

Subconclusion: UCC can be profitable.

194

Question 2

Table 2: Production estimates

	Mon.	Tues.	Wed.	Thurs.	Fri.	Total
Ending stock:						
Cartons	1 368	2 664	3 240	4 320	3 312	
Loose	500e	500e	500e	500e	743	
Daily sales	96	1 440	2 880	2 016	5 400	
Subtotal	1 964	4 604	6 620	6 836	9 455	
Less, begin. stocks:						
Cartons	0	1 368	2 664	3 240	4 320	
Loose	0	500	500	500	500	
Production	1 964	2 736	3 456	3 096	4 635	15 887
"Turns"	3.4	4.7	6	5.4	8	27.5

Table 3: Analysis of yield from raw materials
         (critical material – paraffin)

Paraffin used:

Wax in drums, beginning	150 kg (e)
Wax issued	1 120
Subtotal	1 270
Less: Wax in drums, end	180e
Wax used	1 090
Expected output $\frac{1\ 090}{0.045}$	24 222 candles
Apparent output (table 2)	15 887
Variance	−8 335 (34.4%)

(Possible explanations: high proportion of spilled and wasted wax and/or heavy pilferage of raw materials or finished products.)

Table 4:   Partial pro forma operating statement,
           five days

Sales value of saleable output
    ($\frac{15\ 887}{72}$ x Sh.32.40)   Sh.7 149.15

Raw material costs:

    Paraffin 1 090 kg at Sh.5.60   Sh.6 104
    Thread (200-164) x Sh.0.50   18
    Boxes (50 000-47 000) x Sh.0.15   450
    Cartons (4 000-3 800) x Sh.0.60   120   6 692.00

Margin over materials cost   457.15
Operating costs:

    Gas (assume 2.5) x Sh.55   137.50
    Labour (assume 15) x Sh.7 x 5   525   662.50

Loss before fixed costs   (205.35)
                                                    ======

Question 3

     If students have completed some such analysis as
the above, they should find it easy to recognise the flaw
in Mary's reasoning about the cost of ingredients in
coloured candles.   The relevant cost of salvaged wax is
the amount of extra labour required to salvage it, beyond
that required to clean up for safety reasons.   This may
become one of the bits of "additional information" the
students request in response to question 4.

     Students should discuss the problems of making
coloured candles, such as the need to dedicate one of the
two melting drums to coloured candles, dedicating one or
more kettles and a certain proportion of the frames to
coloured candles, and the additional care required to
keep the white candles free of coloured taints throughout
the process (e.g. women who are trimming and packing
coloured candles may have to work on a different part of
the benches to keep the trimmings clear of the space
where white candles are handled).

Question 4

     If the case is used for only a single class period,
the instructor may want to keep the discussion of additional information purely at the qualitative level.   On
the other hand, particularly if the case is used in an
operations management course, after the students have
discussed the need for additional information, one may

196

want to hand out the case supplement (which is, in fact, an hypothetical set of "observations" generated by the case writer, since such data were not actually gathered in the field). With such additional data students can gain a more detailed understanding of the production process, particularly concerning the capacity constraints represented by the 48 frames and the time required for paraffin to harden satisfactorily.

Question 5

Even without the supplemental information, students may suggest a number of changes, focused on improved productivity or reduced pilferage or both. Steps to improve productivity include investing in a repair job on the roof, bringing in someone to light the burners earlier than 8 a.m., some rearrangements of the flow of work, including breaking through additional doorways or pass-throughs, repositioning one or another of the processes, increasing the number of tea kettles and pourers, placing the moulds side by side rather than end to end to reduce the distance walked, and a number of other reasonably simple actions, none of which intuitively requires a large investment.

A discussion of means to prevent dishonesty can also be kept at a reasonably simple level, because of the building's size and shape. Students might question the placement of the "office", and even question whether the boss should spend much time in his office in this business. Control measures such as daily physical inventories with reconciliation to sales, and particularly a measurement of the salvaged paraffin scraped up from floors and benches are ideas which students should include in a programme.

Question 5 (using supplemental information)

There are many different ways in which the student might organise the supplemental information. One possible way is traced through in this note, in terms of a series of questions which the student asks himself.

(a) Taking the activities involving a frame as a constraint, what is the maximum number of "turns" per 8-hour day?

Activity	Time involved (seconds)		
	Minimum	Maximum	Average
Detail from table C	200	500	330
Wait between passes 1 and 2 (standard inferred from table A)			60
Setting-up time (standard inferred from table A)			1 200
Total			1 590
Total in minutes			26.5

This implies about 17 turns per day as a maximu, with no provision for queues or delays.

(b) Taking the activities involving workers as a constraint, what is the maximum number of "turns" for 15 workers, in an 8-hour day?

Step No. (from table C)	Workers	Unit	Average time (sec.)	Time per turn (worker-min.)
1	2	1 frame	30	48
2	2	"	40	64
3	1	"	60	48
4	1	"	60	48
5	1	2 frames	30	12
6	1	1 frame	35	28
7	1	"	25	20
8	1	2 frames	40	16
9	1	1 frame	30	24
10	1	"	30	24
11	1	2 frames	20	8
12	1	4 frames	180	36
13	1	1 candle	15	144
14 and 15	1	6 candles	25	40
16 and 17	1	72 candles	50	7
18	1	216 candles	30	1
			Total	568

This implies about 12 turns per day, with no provision for delays or personal time for workers. It also assumes complete interchangeability of workers from job to job.

198

(c) Given the fact that 10 turns per day seems to be a profitable level of operation, what would be a reasonable assignment of workers to tasks and areas in which to work?

A number of different assignments can be worked out. One way to simplify the calculations is to conceive of each "cycle" through which four frames would pass (four frames is approximately the number which can be poured from a single kettleful of wax). The pouring time for four frames averages 4 mins. If each pourer gets her own wax, this would call for 7 min. per cycle (or 8 min. to allow for about 12.5% personal time).

Then the various other jobs could be assigned in clusters of activities which added up to approximately 8 mins. per cycle. One such assignment is as follows:

Worker No.	Jobs	Time per cycle (each worker)	Personal time %
1 and 2	Wick preparation	9.3 min.	negative
3 and 4	Wax pouring	7	12.5
5 and 6	Steps 8, 9, 10, 11 (table C)	6	25
7-10	Steps 3, 4, 5 (table C)	5	37.5
11-13	Finishing	8	none
14-15	Packing	4	50

This first pass assignment suggests that workers 7-10 (who are located in the same room with wick twisting) should spend some time in wick preparation. The packers should also help with finishing.

Ideas for the improvement of processes (such as positioning thread spools on spindles so that four threads can be pulled and cut at one time, and perhaps the introduction of a simple hand-drill to impart twist to the wicks) should be encouraged. A major focus of discussion should be on ways to reduce the traffic through the "bottleneck" doors; a good deal could be accomplished by locating "pass through" openings between rooms D and C and rooms C and E. Relocating the frame-stringing operation so that it could be done with merely a "pass-along" of the empty frames after they had been emptied would help cut down both on labour time and confusion.

IV. Classroom use

The case was originally gathered and written for use in a production course in the country of origin. It proved extremely useful, however, as an integrating case bringing production and accounting and control courses together. Because the production process is so inherently simple, the product so familiar and the scale of operations so small, it also was used on occasion as a very early case in general management, where some additional time was given to the marketing policy aspects of the case.

The first year the case was used it arose from a student "consulting" project, and students visited the factory before discussing the case in class. The next year the case was discussed from its written form, and only later on did students visit the factory.

I believe that the teacher should not feel constrained by any sense that large "cultural differences" make this case difficult to deal with out of its context. Interestingly enough, some of the African students wanted to design highly automated (and thus very expensive) alternate processes!   It might be well to emphasise to American students, however, that new machinery of any sort would almost surely have to be imported, and thus would be difficult to justify.   Further, it would be well to point to the evidence in the case about unemployment (almost all the workers were still available to come back when the candle factory was reopened), which, together with the very small impact of wages on the profit statement, suggests that this is not a problem so much of doing away with labour costs as of making sure that existing capital assets are fully utilised.

Abstract

The sales manager of a seeds improvement scheme in a developing country finds that a single order for about 7% of the annual supply of some of his most critical seed products has been mishandled. The scheme has delivered the seeds to a variety of points throughout the country, yet apparently will not receive payment for them. The scheme and its customer are both government-run agencies, and the customer agency is financed largely by a United Nations agency. The sales manager tries to decide on a plan of action.

Possible teaching plan

This case can be used to teach communications, control and decision making, particularly in public administration. Students should be asked first "what should the sales manager do now and why?". Secondly, they may be asked to develop a system which would avoid similar problems in the future.

THE UNWANTED SEEDS

The Tundoro Seeds Improvement Scheme was set up within the Tundoro Department of Agriculture to multiply, and supply the nation's farmers with good improved seeds at reasonable prices. The Scheme dealt with cereal

---

This case was written under the direction of John I. Reynolds. It can be used with Part II of this manual.

seeds: maize, millet and sorgham; legume seeds: groundnuts, beans and soyabeans; and some pasture seeds.

These seeds were supplied to farmers in three ways:
through farmers' unions, through private traders and
directly to some farmers. It was the policy of the
Scheme to supply government-organised bodies such as
research stations, other agricultural programmes and some
corporations first before supplying individual farmers.

Legume seeds - groundnuts, beans, and soyabeans -
were the most difficult to produce because of their low
multiplication factor, susceptibility to destructive
diseases and vulnerability to adverse weather conditions.
Yet they were in great demand. Most legume seeds were
therefore supplied to government-organised bodies; only
a few went directly to farmers.

The Tundoro Young Farmers' Organisation (TYFO) was
organised within the Department of Agriculture but was
financed by the World Food Federation (WFF), an international organisation. In February 1971, an understanding was reached between the officers of the Scheme and
representatives of TYFO/WFF that every growing season,
TYFO/WFF would require the following amounts of seeds to
be delivered directly to the district officers of the
TYFO: 100 packets of groundnuts, 125 packets of soyabeans
and 50 packets of beans (1 packet of groundnuts weighs
24 kg and costs 66/-, 1 packet of beans weighs 6.5 kg and
costs 12/-, and 1 packet of soyabeans weighs 8 kg and
costs 15/60) for each planting season in 4 districts of
Tundoro as shown in exhibit 1.

Exhibit 1

Place	No. of packets		Cost of seeds	Cost of delivery	Total costs
District I	Nuts	100	6 600/-		
	Beans	50	600/-	100/-	9 250/-
	Soya	125	1 950/-		
District II	Nuts	100	6 600/-		
	Beans	50	600/-	80/-	9 230/-
	Soya	125	1 950/-		
District III	Nuts	100	6 600/-		
	Beans	50	600/-	52/-	9 202/-
	Soya	125	1 950/-		
District IV	Nuts	100	6 600/-		
	Beans	50	600/-	20/-	9 170/-
	Soya	125	1 950/-		
Total					36 852/-

That would mean supplying the same amount twice a
year at a total cost of Sh.73,704 or a little over 13% of
total cash inflows to the Scheme for seeds per year.   In
the first season of 1971, this amount was despatched and
payment was duly effected.

In December 1971, the Scheme's sales manager estimated that the amount required by the TYFO/WFF would
involve about 12% of the total cash inflows in 1972.
This was significant in that it was an assured market,
but it would also be a means of extension promotion of
the seeds sales as the TYFO were well supervised by the
agricultural staff, and other farmers would see the good
produce from the seeds.   Consequently the sales manager
visited the TYFO office to ascertain the orders for
1972.   He was informed that the same amount of seeds
delivered for the second season would be required for the
first season of 1972, and should be supplied in early
March.   In January 1972, the officer in charge of TYFO
visited the sales manager and confirmed the orders,
urging timely delivery.   On 14 February 1972, the sales
manager confirmed the acceptance of the orders by letter
to TYFO;   TYFO telephoned to urge timely delivery.   On
3 February 1972, WFF wrote to the sales manager requesting speedy delivery of the seeds.

In the first week of March, the sales manager distributed all the required seeds and informed the TYFO
(copy to WFF) accordingly, by letter dated 13 March 1972.
Then on 15 March 1972 WFF wrote the following letter to
the sales manager:

Thank you for your letter of 13th March,
ref. 880/18, and for the explanation of the double
deliveries of seeds to TYFO.   It is apparent that
there was a misunderstanding.   Originally, WFF
envisaged two planting seasons, but at a meeting
held with the Permanent Secretary/Ministry of
Agriculture, in October 1971, it was appreciated
that 2 planting seasons were proving too onerous
and that in fact second season planting had not
proved favourable .....

Consequently there were no funds available to pay
for the seeds already supplied.   The sales manager was
baffled as he was not aware of the said meeting between
WFF and his permanent secretary and therefore was not
aware of any "double deliveries" he was supposed to have
explained in his letter of 13 March 1972.   He later
learned that the seeds supplied to TYFO in September 1971
for the second season planting were not all planted; some
were stored by TYFO for first season planting in 1972.

This sparked off a series of correspondence between the Scheme and TYFO/WFF. WFF was adamant; they would not release any money for payment for the seeds, and advised that the seeds delivered be collected back by the Scheme. The sales manager refused on the grounds that most of the seeds delivered to the districts were already distributed to the Young Farmers, who had planted them. And the Scheme would not like to meet the cost of collecting the seeds back anyway. In any case it was already too late to redistribute those collected seeds for first season planting. Those legume seeds were very difficult to store for planting in the following season and therefore could hardly be sold at all. The TYFO agreed in principle to pay for the seeds since their farmers had planted them already, but they pointed out that they had no funds available and that it was not likely that any funds would be made available for that payment next financial year.

Thus the Scheme was not only owed Sh.36,852/- (about 7% of the total cash inflows for 1972) but was also likely to lose one of the best ways of extension/promotion of seeds in the future through the Young Farmers. The sales manager therefore wondered what he should do.

Abstract

A participant in a case writers' workshop is trying to decide on which of several situations to focus his attention in order to write a successful case. His case leads differ in respect of the usefulness of the potential case for his uses, the likelihood of his being able to get the needed information, and the likelihood of having the case released after it was written.

Possible teaching plan

This case is best used as part of a case writers' workshop, when the topic of "case leads" is discussed. The group should be asked to decide which one of the leads should be followed up first, which should be used as a "back-up" possibility if the first one falls through, and why. After the case has been discussed the group should be encouraged to discuss their own case leads, in the same terms.

PROFESSOR IGNAZIO'S CASE LEADS

In the fall of 1977 Professor Ignazio returned to his university from a case writers' workshop held in a neighbouring country. He had agreed to write a teaching case to present in February 1978 when the workshop would

---

This case was written by John I. Reynolds as a basis for class discussion and not as an example either of effective or ineffective problem solving. It can be used with Part III of this manual.

reconvene. He had never written a case, although he
occasionally used cases in teaching his course in accounting and control. Professor Ignazio had discussed two
case leads with the workshop leader, Dr. Jonas, and he
knew of several other possible sources of cases. He
must quickly make a decision about where to bend his
efforts in the next few weeks. Because he must add case
writing to his normal teaching load, he could not afford
to waste time in gathering data from a manager who later
refused to sign a release for the case to be used.
Release was important because Dr. Jonas had said that
credit for full completion of the workshop would go only
to those participants who brought fully released cases
to the meetings in February.

Lead No. 1

        Of the two case leads Professor Ignazio had dis-
cussed with Dr. Jonas, he was most confident that he
could gather the material and secure a release on a case
that involved his brother-in-law, Mr. Wroth. Mr. Wroth
was a supervisor in the local electric utility in
University City, and he had often talked to the Professor
about the "antiquated" methods of evaluation used by the
company in granting promotions and raises.

        As he described this situation, Professor Ignazio
had sensed that Dr. Jonas was somewhat cool to the idea.
He noted that Dr. Jonas asked several questions:

        "As a supervisor, could Mr. Wroth find himself in
any difficulty with his superiors because he released
this case, if they later found out about it?" Yes, he
probably could, but couldn't the situation be disguised
so that it could not be traced to Mr. Wroth?

        "Is the electric utility the only such business in
your country?" Yes.

        "Is the company's evaluation scheme unique in any
way because it is a utility?" Professor Ignazio could
not be sure, but thought that it might be.

        "How do you see the case you could write fitting
into your course in accounting and control?" Not
directly, but perhaps in a catchall section where intra-
company relationships came up, if there was time at the
end of the term.

Professor Ignazio had far less information and confidence about release in the instance of the second case lead he discussed with Dr. Jonas. In fact the possibility had arisen only just as he was leaving to go to the workshop, and he had had no chance to follow it up. The lead arose in the following way.

Professor Ignazio had bumped into Joseph Salone at the University City airport as they stood together in a ticket line. Salone had been one of Professor Ignazio's brightest students of a class six years before. When he learned of Professor Ignazio's destination Salone said, "You know that I now run my own accounting firm in my home town, 250 miles from University City. I have always thought that I learned a lot from the cases we studied at the university, but I wished that more of them had dealt with the environment of our own country, rather than the western world. Furthermore, not enough attention is paid to the problems of the small entrepreneur. If you ever get down my way, please drop into my office. I'd come to see you at the university, but my trips to University City are rare, really." This sounded to Professor Ignazio like a somewhat general offer to co-operate with case writing, but Salone had not mentioned any specific problems. In fact, Salone had looked prosperous enough that one might assume he had no problems.

Dr. Jonas, somewhat to Professor Ignazio's surprise, had seemed far more receptive to this case lead than to the former, even though there were almost no details. He asked only three questions:

"How many small accounting firms such as Salone's do you suppose there are in your country?" Probably 50 or more.

"Do you have a section in your course devoted to small accounting firms?" Yes.

"What are the travel arrangements between University City and Salone's home town?" Progressor Ignazio was not sure, but thought there was a least one round-trip plane flight per day.

Other potential leads

During the workshop Dr. Jonas had emphasised that each participant should give a great deal of thought to potential case leads, since there would be too little time to follow up any but the most promising. Professor Ignazio had jotted down the following notes:

"Thompson?"   (Dr. Thompson was an expatriate
faculty colleague of Ignazio's who was the only teacher
in the country, so far as Ignazio knew, who had written
cases.   Thompson, on contract with the university to
teach business policy, had been instrumental in calling
Ignazio's attention to the case writing workshop, and in
persuading the university administration to pay Ignazio's
way to the workshop.   Thompson was consulting for
several local companies, and might be doing case writing,
also, Ignazio supposed.)

"Azuza Brick?"   (The local newspapers were full of
an alleged scandal at the Azuza Brick Company.   It was
said that the company had lost a great deal of money
when their accountant had turned up missing.   Ignazio
belonged to the same local sports club as the president
and several vice-presidents of Azuza.)

"The university accounting system?"   (On several
occasions Professor Ignazio had been asked by the provost
of his university to consult with the administration
about what he called the "archaic and chaotic" system of
accounts of the university.)

"The sports club?"   (There were strong rumours among
the membership of the sports club that an interesting
situation existed in the administration of the club.
Over a drink the current president of the club had told
Ignazio about his disillusionment with the full-time
executive secretary.   Ignazio believed this represented
an excellent human relations case lead, and that his
friend, the president, was fed up enough to release the
case, if it could be properly disguised.)

"Richard's father?"   (Richard Rando had been a
student of Ignazio's for a year, and was enrolled for the
fall term in two of Ignazio's classes.   Richard's
father owned a soft-drink bottling franchise in University City.   Ignazio knew that the international company
which granted Mr. Rando the franchise insisted on instal-
ling its own accounting system, and he believed that a
useful teaching case could be written about the problems
of adapting local accounting systems to international
standard systems.   Richard had suggested on two occasions when he had visited Ignazio's office to discuss his
academic performance, that he would be glad to introduce
Ignazio to his father.   "He would let you write a case
or consult about his problems, I'm sure, Professor.")

"Joseph Koggins?"   (Joseph Koggins was a local man
who was vice-president for finance of the University City
branch of Multinational Enterprises, a maker and seller
of a wide variety of products.   Koggins had been sent
overseas by his form to a management training programme

which had been taught by case method.   This had led to
a contact between Koggins and Ignazio.   Koggins had
visited the university to interview students as prospective employees.   When he heard that Ignazio was teaching
by cases, he had called up to offer, "I'll be glad to
meet with your students informally after a case discussion - perhaps one about transfer pricing problems.   As
you know, that is a topic much in debate between multinational companies and governments, these days."   Ignazio
had not yet taken advantage of Koggins' offer.)

The next step?

Dr. Jonas had told the participants to prepare
quickly a plan of action, including deciding which case
leads to pursue and how far to go before settling on one
lead to follow up in detail.   Professor Ignazio believed
he must "find his case" among the short list of leads he
had jotted down.

Lecturer's note

When this interview was presented to the class
(case writers' workshop participants), the participants
unanimously agreed that it should be edited and released
as a case.   Two reasons were given:

1. That it could be used to clearly bring home to
    students of management or business studies, who are
    usually scared or uninterested in quantitative
    methods, the importance of acquiring such knowledge.
    It is hoped that the admission by a lecturer of her
    need for such competence in that field would stress
    the point.

2. That the interview also highlights two types of
    interviewing skills:

    (i) non-directive, and

    (ii) problem solving.

Possible teaching plan

This case can be used as a part of the introductory
material in a case writers' workshop, when the focus is
on interviewing techniques which are useful for gathering case information.

This case was written in the Nigerian case writing
workshop (1978) by Austin Ejimatswa.   It can be used
with Part III of this manual.

THE INTERVIEW

This interview was an exercise designed to improve the interviewing skill of participants during a three-week case writing workshop, held in one of the States in the western part of the country. The workshop was organised by a federal government institution, charged with management development in the country, with the assistance of the ILO.

The interviewee, Titi Ademoja (Mrs.), an American-trained lecturer in the department of business studies in a higher institution of learning in the country's capital city, holds a bachelor's degree in the social sciences and a master's degree in urban management. The interviewer, James Madugu, works with the federal government institution mentioned earlier and holds a bachelor's degree in the social sciences.

In the absence of a tape recorder, it was not possible to record, verbatim, the words of both the interviewer and interviewee. What has been written is a paraphrase of the interview. (Names used are fictitious.)

James: Good afternoon. It's been sure another brain-jarring day. I can see that you are as tired as I am but let's get done with this interview. Well, what would you like to talk about?

Titi: Good afternoon too. You are right. This workshop is, no doubt, demanding but I suppose one tries to keep up with the high tempo. As for what I would like to discuss with you, what else is uppermost in my mind at this time than the workshop and how I relate to it?

James: What d'you mean? Could you explain further?

Titi: You see, I have been kind of disturbed about the deficiency of my knowledge for this workshop. I am sort of disturbed in the area of quantitative cases. I mean I don't know where to begin, how to begin and how to apply it to policy making or decisions. I feel mixed up. However, I justify this deficiency in my educational background.

James: So you are saying that your academic background has not equipped you with the necessary tools to enable you to handle quantitative cases properly.

Titi: No. It's not exactly that.   It is simply that
         the knowledge is not deep enough.   I have some
         knowledge of the basic concepts of quantitative
         methods.   But I have no confidence in being able
         to tackle cases that require the manipulation of
         figures in analysing them.   I am faced with the
         problem of being able to analyse these cases as
         some colleagues have been doing in this workshop.
         When a colleague analysed what initially seemed
         to be a difficult case, I found it so easy that
         I questioned myself as to why I hadn't thought
         of it before.

James: So you are disturbed about this?

Titi: Yes, of course.

James: But why?

Titi: Management is a field that requires grounding in
         both its quantitative and qualitative aspects.
         And I am not happy about lacking in quantitative
         methods.

James: So you think you need the knowledge in quantita-
         tive methods in order to be a full-fledged
         management educator?

Titi: Well, yes but ...

James: You are sure you need it, why the reservation?

Titi: You see, I have thought of getting one of my
         colleagues back at the college to help in analys-
         ing the quantitative portions of a case while I
         handle the qualitative aspects.   You see, my
         problem is lack of confidence.   But I recognise
         the need to give my students a balanced knowledge
         of management.

James: In other words, you are worried about your
         curriculum and how it will affect your students?

Titi: Yes.   I kind of have this fear of giving my
         students a lopsided knowledge of management.
         Even some qualitative cases involve the manipula-
         tion of figures to be well analysed.   Just like
         the case we treated this afternoon, we analysed
         some figures to locate personnel problems.

James: Since your concern is about your students and
         since you work in a higher institution of learn-
         ing, is it not possible for you to organise your
         curriculum in such a way that you handle mainly

qualitative cases whilst another lecturer handles quantitative cases?

Titi: I don't want to. Apart from giving my students an all-round management education, I need the knowledge of quantitative methods to be able to write good cases.

James: Well, since apparently you know your problem, you want to develop confidence in handling cases with figures, have you thought of possible solutions?

Titi: In the long run, I have thought of going on further studies with emphasis on quantitative methods.

James: In the interim what would you be doing?

Titi: I suppose I will look up some books in our library.

James: Have you thought of getting your colleagues at your workplace to enlighten you?

Titi: That's a good suggestion. I also hope that by going through other cases that I would develop my knowledge.

James: Well, you want the confidence to be able to tackle cases with figures, you hope that by going through cases and reading you would develop your know-ledge. But what efforts have you made before now?

Titi: It's the workshop that has made me to realise this need. I have found that the basic knowledge is just not enough. I have to come to realise the need for a deeper knowledge of quantitative methods in order to be able to confidently and effectively analyse quantitative cases.

James: So, if I've understood you correctly you are dis-turbed by your lack of in-depth knowledge of quantitative methods and consequently lack confid-ence in effectively handling cases with figures. You feel knowledge is important to you as a case writer and teacher; your ambition is to have a deeper understanding of quantitative methods.

Titi: That's right.

James: Thank you. I suppose that, just like you, other participants would discover areas that need improvement in their knowledge.

Abstract

   A young Nigerian business manager (Ukpong) has
invested his own money in machinery to process garri, a
staple food.   His business purpose was to provide
profitable employment for members of his large extended
family.   After a good start the small company had virtually ceased operating.   At the end of the first case
Ukpong is faced with the dilemma of how to proceed without offending the senior member of the family, his
uncle, who has had considerable responsibility for running the company.

   The Stage II case reports the outcome of a meeting
between Ukpong and his uncle, and introduces the thought
that Ukpong might learn from his experience as he plans
for further developments of family enterprise.

Possible teaching plans

   The finished cases (not the drafts shown here) could
be used to introduce students to the special human problems of family enterprise.   A class period could be
devoted to the case, focused on the question, "What
should Ukpong do, and why?"   Near the end of the class
period, the Stage II paper could be handed out and made
the basis for drawing some conclusions about effective
implementation of family relationships.

   These first drafts of cases, however, can be very
effectively used in the teaching of case writing.   After

   This case was written in the Nigerian case writing
workshop (1978) by Martin Asamoah-Manu.   It can be used
with Part III of this manual.

the case writers have studied a number of "finished"
cases, they can confront this draft before starting out
to write their own first cases.   The difficulties the
group will encounter with this draft will suggest the
reasons for several of the conventions about case writing
that are emphaised in the manual:

- writing consistently in the past tense;

- using a first "introductory" paragraph to set the
  scene;

- keeping carefully in mind the "decision point date"
  of the case, so that all information can be brought
  to that point and not beyond it.

Two other points can be brought out here.   One is
that a footnote describing the Nigerian monetary units
and their relationships would help make the case more
widely useful.   The second is that the case writer has
an excellent opportunity to clarify manufacturing processes by giving careful descriptions, and that words
spent in doing so would not be wasted.

The case writers' group could be asked to provide
a detailed prescription for rewriting the case and its
Stage II to improve it as a teaching vehicle.   Because
this case situation was in fact an excellent one for
teaching purposes, and the final case was a very "teach-
able" one, this is a good vehicle for learning how to
rewrite.

FIRST DRAFT

THE EKPO FAMILY BUSINESS ENTERPRISES

Stage I

It is 15 years this year, 1975, since the Ekpo
family took a decision to set up a family business.
Preminent among a number of original aims were the provision of gainful employment for the family members and
the productive utilization of the vast family land.
Ekpo family consists of several lineages.   One of them
is Udo.

Ekpo family is considered to be one of the most
progressive families in the Ikpa Community.   Out of the
family funds, a number of promising members of the family
have been sponsored for further studies in higher institutions at home and overseas.   Those who complete their

216

studies return home to assist in the family effort to train other younger ones. The annual family re-union is a regular feature.

For some three or four annual meetings now, the issue of the 'Ekpo family Enterprises' has featured prominently, but with no concrete decision because of the tendency to wait one more year, hopefully, by then, some more members shall have returned home.

In February, 1975, while on his annual leave at home, Ukpong, 34, a highly educated member of the family, decided that in the absence of other members of the family, he would put the family's long-standing plan - the establishment of the EKPO FAMILY ENTERPRISES-into action. Ukpong, of the Udo lineage, holds a key position in one of the country's finance institutions, located some two hundred kms. away from home. Ukpong consulted his uncle, Ette, on the issue. Ette, the present Ekpo family head, after many years as a school master, was working in one of the ministries in the State Capital, some sixty kms. away. Ette visited home very regularly, where the younger of his two wives, Eno, lived and taught in the village school. Thus, it was possible for Ukpong to meet Ette at home on Ukpong's annual leave to discuss his (Ukpong's) plan to start the family business. Ette was most impressed with Ukpong, and subsequently gave his wholehearted support:

> "But my nephew," Ette intoned "as you know, at the moment, I cannot help much financially, but leave all matters on personnel to me. You and I are based away from home. I will instruct my wife, Eno, the teacher, to supervise the whole operation. You go back to the city and put all these decisions on paper."

Thus, the Ekpo Family Enterprises was born with garri processing factory as the first project.

Garri processed out of the cassava tuber plant, is an important stable food for a sizeable percentage of the entire Nigerian population. But for the Ikpa Community where the factory was sited, garri plays a unique role; it is the staple food. There are other meals, but they are never alternatives. There may be supplementaries, but never substitutes to garri. A day without garri meal is considered traditionally as fasting. Until Ukpong conceived the idea, producing garri in the community and other communities within eight kms. radius, had been on household basis.

Ikpa community is centrally placed among some fourteen other villages, each with a little over one thousand inhabitants.   The next commercial centre, Ukam, is nearly fifteen kms. away.   For Ikpa community, a journey to Ukam is always to be dreaded because of the many lives that have been lost on the canoe trip.   The recent introduction of motor boats - though fast and accidents less frequent - yet when they do occur, they simply are ghastly.   Most of the senior members prefer to go to Ukam on foot, an additional eight kms.

One other reason why the Ikpa community were willing to accept the processed garri was the great reduction in the time of laborious traditional method of preparing garri.   Traditionally, after the raw cassava has been harvested from the farms, its hard brown outer skin is peeled off.   It is then grated manually.   Next, it is put in a bag and pressed to remove a lot of its juice (liquid).   This is the first phase of dehydration process.   It is allowed a day before roasting.   This includes the process of separating rough roots from the nicer finer texture.   Next, the finer texture is thoroughly fried.   This is the second and final phase of dehydration.   It is ready for sale.   Preparation of about five kilograms of garri from the first dehydration stage to the end can take a whole day.   Ukpong's factory could go through all these processes - from peeling stage to frying stage-in just about twenty minutes.   On the average, thirty people are served each day.   Processing fee per "standard basket load" is about fifty kobo.   An unskilled labourer is paid about two naira per day.

In 1965, 10-12 cigarette tinfuls of garri sold for one shilling (ten kobo).   In 1977, the same quantity sells for one naira - about one thousand percent increase in a decade.

At that important meeting of Ukpong and Ette, it was decided that Ukpong was to provide about ninety per cent of the initial capital.   Labour was the responsibility of Ette.   Profits were to be equally shared between Ukpong and Ette.   Other members of the family now abroad, were to be welcome to join in as they returned home.   Eno was to be the chief executive on a minimum part-time pay of ₦25.00 monthly.   Ukpong purchased the garri processing plant and other relevant equipment consisting of a 3 horse-power diesel engine, a twin cassava grater/palm kernel cracker.   Ukpong's initial expenditure was ₦2,500.00.   All receipts were written in Ukpong's name.

Ette, however, was unable to convince any of the family youngersters to assist in the enterprise initially. Several excuses were given.   Ette therefore had to resort to hired labour at the government rate of ₦2.00 per day per head.   Six labourers were employed initially.

218

In late March, 1975, the Ekpo Family garri factory
started operation for the first time.   Response was very
high.   Ukpong, because of his training, had provided a
simple book-keeping exercise book.   But neither Eno, nor
the six other employees saw much need for that book.
Ime, the most promising of the six employees, had initially attempted to put down some basic facts.   For some two
months Ette wrote fairly regularly to Ukpong.   In those
letters Ette attempted to give periodic reports but they
were too general to be really useful.   Ukpong's first
visit home was some four months later.   Eno had much to
report, though only orally.   The way she presented her
accounts left Ukpong unimpressed.   For example, she declared ₦75.00 as profit for the period, but Ukpong realized that ₦12.00 diesel bought about a month earlier,
had not been paid for, one labourer was yet to collect
his pay of ₦9.00, one other labourer had overdrawn his ˋ
pay by ₦6.00

Five family members have joined the operation.   No
mention was made of how much to pay them.   With the im-
volvement of the other family members, Ukpong had hoped
for the better.   He did not effect any changes before he
returned to his base.   He planned major changes in his
next visit.   The project, however, had brought life into
the family, in particular, and the community as a whole.
With the unexpected initial progress, five hitherto
uncommitted members of the family gave up their less productive occupations and joined the family enterprise.
The community folks were happy that the Ekpo family had
saved them the daily 10 kms. walk to the nearest cassava/
palm kernel processing plant.

Due to pressure of work, Ukpong could not visit home
until his next annual vacation leave in February, 1976.
For some six months prior to his visit, Ukpong did not
receive any report.   When he arrived, he found a very
low level of activity.   Some time ago, at least 50 standard baskets of garri were processed each day at 50k each,
but now, for days, there would be no attendants at the
factory to attend to the many customers.   Grievances
were rampant, mainly against Eno's supervisory style.
Eno, on the other hand, accused Ime, and two of the family
members of "illegal deals with customers."

Three of the five family members resigned; so did
eight of the hired labourers.   Though all the machinery
and equipments were still active, there was less then
₦50.00 to show for nearly eight months of operation.   The
issue of how much to pay the family members who left was
still outstanding.   As at February, 1976, Ukpong had
realized less than 15% of his capital outlay (approx.
₦300.00 of the ₦2,500.00 expended).

Ukpong's private investigations revealed that the project assumed a downward trend soon after the supervisor had maltreated Ime, the hard-working machine operator. Ime left without notice. Ukpong asked for a meeting with Ette and Eno for following Sunday:

> " - all the signs point to Eno, as the cause of the ills of the business. But one does not need to come from my home to exercise caution in such a situation. For one thing, Ette had asked me to settle, privately, the issue of Eno maltreating Ime." Ukpong reminded himself, among other things.

Ukpong was preparing to take the most appropriate position, bearing in mind the circumstances of the case.

Stage II

After a careful reflection on the factors at play in the Ekpo Family Business Enterprises (Project One), Ukpong came to the conclusion that the major reason why he, one of the youngest in the family, is now at the centre of affairs, was that 99% of the initial capital outlay had come out of his pocket.

> "Under normal conditions," Ukpong said, "this would have been an enviable position to hold on to. However, all the signs point to Eno, as the cause of the ills of the business. But one does not need to come from my home to exercise caution in such a situation. For one thing, Ette had asked me to settle, privately, the issue of Eno maltreating Ime."

At the meeting Ette reminded Ukpong and Eno that the purpose for which the project was set up, and with that declared the meeting open.

Ukpong, taking caution from Ette's brief introduction, stated that there were two alternatives open to them:

A) After calculating the present worth of the project, to share out the assets proportinately, and wind up the business.

B) Either you, Ette, take over the whole business or I do.

The conciliatory attitude of Ukpong impressed his uncle so much that he decide on the latter. He offered to pay for Ukpong's share which amounted to about ₦2,000.00, excluding the ₦300.00 already realized by

220

Ukpong.   Ette would become the sole proprietor.   Ette
informed Ukpong that two of Ukpong's senior brothers had
written from overseas that they were just about returning
home, and that as soon as they arrived, the family enterprise could be reorganized in the most appropriate way.

On that note, the meeting ended.   Ukpong, on the
other hand, picked up the hint and began to do the
groundwork in preparation for Phase 2 of the Ekpo Family
Enterprises, bearing in mind the experience gained from
Phase I.

In September 1969, the faculty of a recently formed graduate school of management in the Philippines organised a seminar to explore the case method. The decision to establish the new school, the design of its curriculum, and the statements of its objectives had been strongly influenced by men who had association with "a well-known university on the east coast of the United States". As a result, the case method was frequently mentioned, case research was one of its scheduled activities, and cases were being used extensively in its courses.

At the same time there seemed to be among faculty members some undercurrent of doubt about what "this case method really is" and how and to what extent it suited the requirements of the school. It was to explore questions such as these that the seminar was set up. A committee of the faculty invited Dr. James W. Culliton to be leader of the first seminar session.

This case can be used with Part IV of this manual.

Culliton, who was then a member of the faculty of the well-known school, was in the Philippines as an adviser on graduate business education under a Ford Foundation Grant. He had had long association with the case method as a student, research assistant (case writer), case writing director, teacher and dean. He told the committee, "I have always felt that there was something paradoxical about a lecture on the case method". He proposed, therefore, that he prepare some notes - a "case" - which would be distributed in advance to the members of the seminar to serve as the basis for discussion. He admitted that, to some extent, this was a gesture to make him feel comfortable because he wished to use the "democratic in distinction to the telling method".[1]

The notes which Culliton prepared are reproduced herewith:

"The first fact (or is it an opinion?) that I'd like to put before you is that there is no such thing as the case method. The term has many different meanings - at least as many as there are people using it, and probably more.

"What I propose to do therefore is to make a number of observations which may have some relevance to an understanding of this multifaceted thing. I have not, in the scholarly sense, researched or documented these observations nor have I made any heroic attempt to structure them into a logical or pseudological pattern. To some extent this may be attributed to laziness on my part but, more to the point - I hope - I am being consistent with my earlier observation that there is no such thing as the case method. Consequently, even if I wanted to try I couldn't tell you what it is - and being a "case man" myself I probably would not <u>tell</u> you even if I thought I knew.

"As I was trying to decide what observations to make I did come up with one idea or hypothesis that has influenced the selection and sequencing of my comments. The hypothesis is that too much attention has been paid to

---

[1] This was a phrase used by Professor Charles I. Gragg in an oft-quoted article "Because Wisdom Can't Be Told", 9-451-005, in which he told some of his wisdom concerning the case method.

the question: "What is the case method?" and that perhaps a more productive question to start with would be "Why is the case method?"

"For this reason, I am going to start with some historical observations and then let them lead where they will to some other characteristics or points of interest.

"It is hard - it is almost impossible - to talk about the case method in business education without talking about Harvard Business School. So, let's start there:

"Harvard Business School was founded in 1908. It wasn't the first school of business established by a reputable educational institution, but it was among the first. Also, it was established at the very beginning exclusively as a Graduate School. Neither it, nor Harvard College, has ever got involved in undergraduate business education. Whether this was for well-thought-out reasons or was a fortuitous event I have never really found out - but I think it is a relevant fact. (By making this statement here I do not want to imply - on the contrary I want to avoid implying - what the relevance is.)

"The first dean of HBS was Edwin Gay. I never knew him personally but learned something about him from my friend Doc Copeland who, while he may not technically have been on the first faculty, was closely associated with the School from its beginning. In his article[1] Doc makes two points I'd like to call to your attention:

"1. Dean Gay - from the very beginning - wanted Commercial Law to be taught by the case method and said that in other courses an analogous method emphasising classroom discussion would be used 'as far as practicable'.

"2. In his own course in Economic History in Harvard College Professor Gay did not practise what he preached.

"Dramatic growth and development of the case method at HBS took place under the second dean, Wallace B. Donham (1911-1942). Dean Gay had been influenced by the

---

[1] Referring to "The genesis of the case method in business instruction", by Melvin T. Copeland in McNair (ed.): The case method at the Harvard Business School (New York, McGraw-Hill, 1954), pp. 25-33.

success of the case method at Harvard Law School (where it had been an innovation).   The Harvard Law School had, in fact, also been used by many young men as a path to business careers.   Dean Donham himself was a Harvard Law School graduate.   Thus there were several influences of law cases on business cases.   But, law had two things business did not have: (1) court cases with decisions, and (2) a reporting system.

"Being the kind of man he was, Donham was not deterred by such obstacles and decided to have HBS set up its own reporting system.

"At this stage of the story, I get somewhat conflicting impressions about what happened.   There were two different approaches - and for our purposes this is more important than historical accuracy of specific events.   One approach, borrowing heavily from the court reporting system, was to collect factual cases as they occurred.   The other was to seek out cases which had some common theme which would develop a course, say, in marketing, production, or accounting.

"At one time, the Bureau of Business Research was the case collecting agency of the School.   While even this system seemed to have some area-oriented programmes there appeared to be a kind of overriding concept that a 'reporting section' would furnish the teaching materials for the School.

"For reasons which need not be explored here, this central reporting system broke down and fairly early in its history case collection became strongly oriented toward case research for specific courses.   As a matter of administrative procedure there was almost an ambivalence between the need for keeping some kind of budgetary and personnel controls over the case collecting activities of the School as a whole and the case research needs of course-oriented professors.

"But, I'm getting a little ahead of my story from a different and important point of view.   When HBS started in 1908 almost no 'body of business knowledge' existed to be taught.   True, there had been some developments along the line of 'scientific management' (say, Taylor, whose <u>Principles and Methods of Scientific Management</u> came out in 1911, or Gantt, whose <u>Work, Wages and Profits</u> was published in 1910);   accounting and commercial law (as Dean Gay mentioned) were quite well structured;   and even penmanship was sometimes mentioned as a business subject.   But the embryonic School did not have a full-blown alternate choice question of which way to <u>teach</u> a body of knowledge as the question sometimes gets posed now.   Since almost no material was available it was probably true that the preparation of material of any kind - even texts or description - would require some research into what was going on in business.

"Another concurrent development reinforces this impression: the Bureau of Business Research got interested in collecting data on the cost of doing business especially in retail operations like hardware, jewellery, and eventually department stores and variety chains. One of the first things the researchers discovered was that nobody in these businesses had much of an idea of what his costs were and, even more importantly from a research standpoint, there were no commonly accepted practices with respect to accounting. So, to get data that had some meaning they had to devise a common reporting system. But this was not superimposed; it grew out of field work. Such field work was not case research as such to produce teaching cases. But it had what we would now call a feedback effect by making a strong impression on the researchers that there weren't any 'best practices'; there weren't any right answers; and, most certainly, there weren't any authoritative answers (like the court decisions of the law cases).

"So, case collecting and case writing began. It wasn't easy. Businessmen weren't in the habit of sharing their information (or even their ignorance). Many of the early cases were short, sketchy. But cases got written and were used in the classroom. Then, their usefulness began to emerge in several ways:

- cases did furnish teaching material;

- cases were realistic (in a way);

- cases got students involved;

- cases opened avenues of thought and research (especially for faculty members);

- cases kept the faculty 'in touch' (sometimes later, I beleive, the analogy to medical schools and their clinics began to be made).

"As I have mentioned several times, business cases, unlike law, had no answers. It seems there were two basic ways to deal with this: (a) try to get expert opinion or consensus, or (b) adopt the open-ended approach.

"Although, as Doc Copeland mentions in his article, some small case books were put out around 1920 (or a little earlier), the first intensive publishing effort seems to have been the <u>Harvard Business Reports</u>.

Volume I, which was published in 1925, had almost no order; no comments. The second volume had a beginning of order plus commentaries by Harvard faculty members. The whole series included 11 volumes, the last of which was published in 1932. The last three were on very specific subjects: Industrial Marketing, Marketing Airplanes and Co-operative Advertising. Even these were not however course oriented as we now think of case books. I view this activity as an attempt to adopt the court reporter system. The consensus seems to be that it didn't work. As a matter of fact the whole experiment was called by one observer 'a debacle'.

"Meanwhile courses began to be more clearly defined as part of a programme of instruction for a School of Business Administration. By this I mean the faculty went beyond just trying to adopt available stuff that would fill up a two-year time period. Conscious effort was made to design a programme. The early course/curricula structures were simple. Even when I started as an MBA student in 1932 the first year consisted of Marketing, Industrial Management, Finance, Accounting and Statistics, plus weekly written reports (but not WAC[1] – the reports were in the basic courses). The second-year programme required Business Policy (but there were, at the time, two substantially different offerings, either of which fulfilled the requirement). It also offered advanced courses in the first-year areas and courses in areas in which certain faculty members had a special interest. Many of these latter courses tended to come and go.

"Thus, case collection became closely associated with course development and by and large has remained so. This inter-relationship led to certain habits or what might be called 'conventions' which were generally accepted:

- case should be real, not armchair;

- business confidence had to be maintained (hence the requirement for a signed release);

- some kind of control of research contacts became necessary;

---

[1] WAC is the abbreviation for a course "Written Analysis of Cases" which evolved later. It not only assigns cases on which students write reports, and grades the reports, but also gives instruction in analytical and writing techniques.

228

- cases should be well written; they were usually submitted to professional editing and were written in the past tense;

- business was offered no 'quid pro quo', BUT ...;

- at the early stages, most cases were <u>issue cases</u>. Then later, diagnostic cases were added; these were followed by experiments in what might be called 'appraisal' cases because of a predeliction on the part of students (nurtured by the climate) always to find something wrong;

- case research was an on-going never-ending process.

"I'd like to conclude these remarks with reference to the Summer Case Writing Program conducted at Harvard several years ago under a Ford Foundation Grant for (I think it was) five summers. Each summer about 40 faculty members from other schools were brought together to study the case method. They observed cases being used in regular programmes at Harvard, they wrote at least one case in their own field of specialisation, some Harvard faculty members led case discussions for them, and they each 'taught' their own case with their own group as students.

"It was this programme which was largely responsible for the establishment of the Intercollegiate Case Clearing House. The main reason I mention it however is to give me the excuse to tell of two incidents:

"1. Just about a month ago I was visited by an alumnus of this programme who is now working in Pakistan in a Ford programme which is smaller than but not dissimilar from the Philippine Program.[1] He has found it useful to distinguish among three aspects of the case method: (a) case research, (b) case writing, and (c) case teaching. I would further subdivide the third aspect into (1) the construction of courses from cases, and (2) the use of cases in the classroom.

---

[1] The "Philippine Program" referred to an Intercollegiate Program of case collection in the Philippines in which the participants were the Asian Institute of Management, Ateneo de Manila University, De La Salle College, University of the Philippines and consultants from the Harvard Business School known as the Harvard Advisory Group (HAG). In a three-year period, 1966-1969, the local faculties together with HAG had produced some 240 cases which were available through the Philippine Case Clearing House, Inc.

"2. In addition to the 'case' kind of work the
Harvard Summer Program also had (paradoxically?) visiting lecturers. One of these was a very dynamic speaker
who took as his topic 'There is no learning without
pain'. His argument was that learning means change and
change is difficult and painful. He argued that the
case method was ideally suited to this painful process.
But he lectured with extreme forcefulness and, in many
different skilful ways, brought home the point: 'There
is no learning without pain'.

"When he had finished, two of the visiting professors rushed from their seats to say to him: 'Doctor, we
enjoyed that very much'."

EDITOR'S NOTE:

What has been the effect to date of Philippine
cases on courses in Philippine business education?

What effect will (or should) Philippine case collection have in the future? On courses? On classroom
instruction? On curricula?

Should Philippine case collection be carried on?
At what pace? At what cost? By whom?

In the fall of 1969 Dr. Culliton, at the request of
the professor in charge of a course in one of the
graduate business programmes in Manila, was reviewing the
first draft of several cases written by two research
assistants. As he was noting his reactions and making
editorial suggestions on the rough drafts, Culliton con-
cluded that there were certain patterns to his observations. In order to prepare for a scheduled conference
with the case writers, he went to the blackboard on his
office wall and sketched some of the ideas that seemed to
come to the forefront.

Exhibit 1 is a copy of what he put on the board.

Later, he spent more than an hour with the two
writers going over their cases in detail but also making
use of the notes on the board. Before he got down to
specifics however he made the following observations:

"1. As you will discover, I am going to be very
frank with you and, on the whole, my comments will appear
to be critical. The reason for this is that I presume

This case was put together by a Philippine Case
Clearing House, Inc., staff member. It was prepared as
a basis for class discussion. Cases are not designed
to present illustrations of either correct or incorrect
handling of administrative problems.

Distributed by the Intercollegiate Case Clearing
House, Soldiers Field, Boston, Mass. 02163, under No. 9-
373-614. All rights reserved to the contributors.
Printed in the USA. This case can be used with Part III
of this manual.

<u>Exhibit 1</u>:   <u>The case method (C)</u>

<u>"Ideas" on cases</u>

I.   Cases should be student-oriented

    A.   Objective

        1.   Analytical experiences   (Not a vehicle for
                                      teaching a
        2.   Feeling of   concept)
            responsibility   (Not an illustra-
                                        tion)
        3.   Need for action but   (Not an exercise)
            not "right" answers

    B.   The student as the reader.   Techniques.

II.   Believability.   Past tense.   Active voice.

III.   Telling vs. Letting the students dig.

IV.   Editorialising.

V.   Opinion vs. Fact.

VI.   Facts of business vs. Artificial issue.

VII.   Bases for selecting and sequencing information.

VIII.   Cases and technical notes.

<u>Source</u>:   Culliton's blackboard.

232

we are all interested in getting the best possible cases. As a result nothing we say to each other about a case or the way it was originally drafted is personal. Incidentally, this is the way I was brought up. It is what I consider fundamental to an academic or scholarly approach and, when I was first getting started in the case writing business myself, I was under some of the toughest mentors in the world.

"2. There is a certain amount of subjectivity in my remarks because from my tutors and from my own experiences over the years I have developed certain attitudes and certain concepts of whay makes a good case. I'll try to let you know when I am aware of strong personal feelings, and where others hold different opinions.

"3. There is no 'best way' to write a case. There are basic and subtle inter-relationships among: the sources of materials and their right to confidentiality which may require disguise; the material itself and the total contents of a course; the plans of the professor for the use of the material; and the stage of the student's development in terms of knowledge and abilities. All these have a bearing on how a particular case should be written. I feel, however, that after all these things are considered, there still remains the need for the case writer himself to maintain his own integrity and the integrity of the case itself."

Culliton then went over the several cases individually with the two research assistants explaining his specific comments - which ranged all the way from minor editorial suggestions in sentence structure to proposed major revisions in the approach to the case. From time to time he related such comments to the points listed in exhibit 1. For purposes of this case, however, his elaboration on the points are given in the order in which the points appear in the exhibit.

"Cases should be student-oriented: This is important from several points of view. The first is associated with a basic aspect of the case method which is that over a period of time a student is faced with many different case situations, no one of which can do all the jobs but all of which together take on new meaning. Some major objectives of cases are: (1) to give the student analytical experiences; (2) to give him a feeling of the kind of responsibility which rests upon real decision makers; and (3) to serve as a constant reminder of the responsibility of somebody to take action but that, while the objective is to achieve better rather than worse action, it is not to teach right answers.

"These same points can be made from a negative point of view: a case is <u>not</u> a vehicle for teaching a concept which the teacher thinks a student should learn; <u>not</u> an illustration; <u>not</u> an excuse for having the student perform an exercise. [Here is one spot where my prejudices may be showing.]

"Secondly, in the preparation of a particular case, the writer should be careful to consider the student as the user of the case. If the facts of the situation are not clear to him the case is a failure. This means that the structure of the case - its beginning, its sequence, its conclusion - must make sense to a reader whom we can usually presume is unfamiliar with the facts to start with. Certain techniques of writing - such as rigid use of topic sentences and paragraph unity (sometimes but not always 'transitional words and phrases') - help to show the reader why you want him to read what comes next. Skilful selection and mixing of sentence lengths and structure also help.

"In my experience, when a well-written case is used in the classroom, the students soon stop talking about 'the case' and become immersed in the situation that the case is about. This is a kind of humbling experience, perhaps, for a case writer because the better job he does the less his work is noticed. Very few people will say 'That is a well-written case' although they will complain about a confusing one.

"It is in this context that '<u>believability</u>' becomes important: if a student is being asked to 'face up to' a situation like a business executive, he should without straining his credibility feel that the situation is one that a business executive has faced or is facing or will face. It ought not be contrived or wishy-washy. The next list of specifics evolved out of basic concerns like these.

"<u>Past tense</u>. <u>Active verbs</u>. Decision-making situations are very active and challenging. Experience has shown that accurate descriptive language in the past tense keeps situations current more than writing them in the present tense. Present-tense writing has to be dated to be accurate and becomes outdated like yesterday's newspaper. Problems and decision making are the things that make an executive's job. If it were not for these, there would be no need for the executive. It is not only dulling but unreal, therefore, to use passive verbs like 'It was decided' or 'only one product was handled by the company'.[1]

"Telling vs. Letting the students dig raises some very interesting questions. Essentially there are three ways to present data: in tables, in charts, and in prose. In one case you (the case writer) have paraphrased in words parts of what has been presented in an exhibit (in figures). This might mean that you are merely repeating the information in different form and whether this is desirable or not depends on many things. For instance, it goes beyond the form in which the data probably came to the decision maker but may save students' time if the professor has some other objective. Or the purpose may be to have the student check certain summary statements against the original data both for accuracy and meaning. If the summary statements had been made by a character in the case (and were so labelled) this may lead to valuable analytical experience. If, on the other hand, the summary was made by the case writer it may constitute a very subtle form of editorialising.

"Editorialising by a case writer, in my opinion, should be avoided and this takes a very conscious effort because editorialising is frequently subconscious. For instance: 'The company was a typical family enterprise', or 'Mr. X was an excellent sales manager', 'Trucking of sugar cane could not have come at a more inopportune time'.

"Opinion vs. Fact is closely associated with editorialising and frequently can be avoided by similar techniques. One is to ascribe the opinion to someone who held it. In this way the fact that the opinion was held becomes doubtly useful, first, in appraising the worth of the opinion, second, in better understanding the person who held it.

"Facts of business vs. Artificial issue. This note is closely associated with several of the above points such as believability, opinion vs. fact, and editorialising. I find such openings as 'Mr. ....,

---

[1] I am painfully aware of the dangers of putting suggestions about writing into writing because most readers are tempted to see how well the preacher practises what he preaches. For instance, much of this 'case' is in the present tense and includes some passive verbs. I dodge the first charge by using the trick of quotes; the second I admit but with the excuses: 'Well nobody's perfect' and 'Good writing requires a change in pace'.

president of ...., was concerned with making
a plan to reorganise the sales department' weak and un-
exciting. Another frequent substitute for 'was concerned with' is 'was working hard on'.

"In my opinion, business executives in responsible
positions ought to be and usually are 'concerned' and
'working hard'. What they are concerned with flows out
of the facts and their own abilities and (many times)
predilections. The business facts which gave rise to
the concern or the hard work are usually more realistic
in terms of cases for student analysis than generalised
statements which seem to try to set up 'an issue' for
the student to focus his attention on in 'this case'.
There are many subtleties in this area and, although
there is no one answer, I think that one extremely useful
norm is integrity. If the case starts out: 'On such-
and-such a date, Mr. President received a memorandum from
the sales manager' or 'called a meeting of his department
heads' these are most likely good starting points IF, in
fact, such an event did take place. If, on the other
hand, it is a fiction created by the case writer to set
up an excuse for dragging in information, most of the
time believability will suffer, the case writer will find
difficulty in relating the data in the case to the
excuse, and eventually the unreality will be discovered
(or felt) by the student. The simple answer is: 'Tell
it like it is'. But, like many simple answers, case
writers will have difficulties in applying it.

"Basis for selecting and sequencing information.
Most business problems are part of an ongoing reality.
How to break into this realistically; how to furnish
the student the necessary background to understand and
deal with the present situation; how to give the student
a feel for the reason why certain information is presented; how to have what is necessarily a small part of
a big picture seem to be self-contained or manageable;
how to decide what information to put in; and even more
difficult, how to decide what information to leave out,
are all part of the art of case writing.

"Most of my earlier comments have some bearing on
this question and no rules of thumb will solve it. I
will merely add a few random observations:

"One of the rules of journalism helps. The first
time a new character or a new idea appears it ought to
have some self-contained explanation of its relevance.
For instance a sentence quoted above: 'Trucking of sugar
cane could not have come at a more inopportune time'
appeared in the middle of a case and there had been no
previous reference to the trucking of sugar cane. It not
only was an important happening (with respect to the

company's problem) but also had certain technical aspects which a student had a right to have explained to him.

"There has been a tendency in the case writing process for cases to become longer and longer. A case writer runs into a very difficult dilemma here. If a student is to have 'all the facts' (which is an impossibility) a case tends to become 'long'. If, on the other hand, he is to be given only relevant facts the case writer (or the professor) assumes the responsibility of deciding what is relevant and, if he is not careful, ends up by deciding what to teach in a particular case. At its extreme this runs counter to certain other objectives of the case method.

"More often than not, in my experience, a clear and realistic statement of what the executive actually was up against is a very effective guideline in determining what belongs in and out of a particular case. Also, my personal preference is to keep cases relatively short by favouring the omission rather than the inclusion of doubtful material. This problem also has a bearing on the next item."

Cases and technical notes. It so happens that all the cases being reviewed by Culliton with the two research assistants dealt with various entities in the sugar industry. Principally because the set of cases was being reviewed as a package (rather than at separate times which is frequently the situation) duplication of background information became readily apparent. He commented: "If this set is viewed from the student's point of view a professor who used the cases as a series might run the risk of boring the student to death because of the repetition of similar facts. One answer to this is to present an 'industry note' into which basic information relevant to many situations will be gathered together. Some of the elements which must be considered here are: (a) whether, in fact, a set of cases on the same industry is to be included in a course so that an industry note becomes economical; (b) the risk that an industry note might become purely descriptive and either bland, on the one hand, or biased on the other; (c) the risk that a note might be only superficially relevant to the decision-making aspect of the individual cases. Here is another place where my prejudices show but, in my opinion, one of the by-products of the case method is the development of student initiative in getting relevant facts thereby enhancing both his decision-making abilities and his general erudition. The tendency to use many technical notes suggests to me that a professor may not really believe in the case method and wishes to exert greater control than it provides over what a student should know and think about."

Appendix A contains the first draft of a case prepared for possible inclusion in a course in Human
Behaviour in Organisation.

It is reproduced with the permission of the author
for use by seminar participants. (Note the draft of
the case is triple spaced to allow for easy correction.)

1. Read the case and indicate (a) what "obvious" change
    you would make in it, and (b) where you have "key
    questions" about the way the case should be written.

2. Prepare a set of instructions for a case writer to
    follow in rewriting the case.

This case was put together by a Philippine Case
Clearing House, Inc. staff member. It was prepared as
a basis for class discussion. Cases are not designed to
present illustrations of either correct or incorrect
handling of administrative problems.

This case can be used with Part III of this manual.

THE CASE METHOD (D)

First draft   HBO _____

BERT ANGELES

January 15, 1969

Dear Pepito,

A couple of months ago, I wrote you about a decision which I may have to make regarding a change in my present employment.   Remember that large American Company here in the Philippines which I mentioned in my last letter? Well, this Company's No. 2 executive, Mr. John Smith, gave me a call this morning offering me the job of Employee Relations Manager, an executive position in the Personnel Department of his Company.   Mr. Smith offered me a salary that is twice my present basic pay in the management consulting firm where I am now employed. Considering that I am presently receiving a fairly good amount in four figures, the offer is quite a substantial increment.   Mr. Smith emphasised that his Company's need

240

for an Employee Relations Manager is rather urgent.   I

agreed to meet with him next week to give my answer, one

way or another.

While I have previously studied this matter and

consulted with some of my close friends, I still do not

know if I should accept the offer or not.   I have been

with my present Company for five years.   I have pro-

gressed in pay and position many more times than I had

expected.   The executives to whom I report have

repeatedly communicated to me and confirmed their acknow-

ledgement of my good performance and potential in the

Company.   As a matter of fact, I have just been recom-

mended for a firm scholarship to the country's top gradu-

ate school in business.   I will get full pay while

studying.   Of course, there is an obligation to spend a

certain number of years with the Company upon graduation,

which I estimate to be at least ten years considering my

rate of pay and the cost of this education.   As you

know, my present employer is a leading and very prestigious firm in its field not only in the Philippines but
in South-East Asia.

Should I accept Mr. Smith's offer, I certainly will
be taking a risk.   I am quite happy with my record as a
consultant, but I do not know how relevant my qualifications and experiences are to this new job.   I have a
Bachelor's degree in Psychology from a university in
California.   Although the type of jobs I have been
handling as a consultant have dealt mostly with personnel
and organisational studies of various companies, I have
never really been exposed to the task of implementing and
living with my recommendations on a day-to-day basis and
this is something I want to try.   It is quite important
that I perform well as an Employee Relations Manager
because I cannot afford a black mark in my record.   This
would make it very difficult for me to get another job
for a salary that is at least equal to that being offered

to me by Mr. Smith.   Personnel jobs are not that highly

rated in other companies.   When I think of my responsi-

bilities as a family man, I find it all the more diffi-

cult to make a decision.

To complicate matters, I forgot to mention to you

that at present, this American Company has a Filipino

executive who has been in the Company for over ten years

as Labor Relations Manager.   He handles mainly manage-

ment-union affairs, although he also performs some other

related aspects of personnel administration.   I have met

this man and I know he has been hoping that the Company

will reward him for his long years of service, by making

him head of all the personnel and labour relations func-

tions in the Company - possibly at a Vice Presidential

level like his contemporaries in the Company.

The other main factor is the probability that my

growth in the Company I'm considering to join will be

rather limited because of my formal training (which is

not in business) and the function I'll be performing.

Personnel functions in most companies tend to have a very

limited scope.   In this American Company none of the

top executives came from personnel.   Compare this to the

potential varied jobs I may be assigned to handle in my

present Company and a chance to obtain a Master's degree

in Business Administration which in the Philippines is

fast becoming an institutional and a basic requirement for

executive and managerial positions.   If you don't have

this MBA degree now and especially in the years to come,

it will be tough to survive.

The third factor is rather personal.   How do I tell

my present bosses, who have been lining me up for more

responsibilities and higher positions in the Company,

that I have decided to leave after all.   You know how we

tend to be too personalistic and sentimental in dealing

with each other even in a business setting.   How do I

convince them that the offered position and the other

Company are both worth joining without sounding ungrateful and causing a strain in our relationships which I cannot afford to ignore considering the influence these individuals can bring to bear upon my prospective employer and other companies.

<u>"Case writing" workshop for</u>
<u>management educators and trainers</u>
(information note)

General information

This workshop grew out of the recognition of the
need for ....[1] based teaching materials. The
workshop is designed for management educators and
trainers in universities, polytechnics, management training and consulting institutions and enterprises who want
to improve their ability to prepare and use local case
materials.

Eligibility

To be eligible, participants should have some case
writing experience (i.e. should have written a case or
participated in a previous case writing workshop). However, consideration will be given to those with little
or no case writing experience but who by their background
and interest can benefit from the programme.

Immediate objective

The case writing workshop is an intensive programme
designed to develop .... management cases and
other teaching materials. The aims of the programme
include:

---

[1] Country name to be completed.

1. Providing guided experience to management educators and trainers in case writing, selection and use.

2. Forming a link between the (sponsoring organisation) and the .... case writers to promote the preparation and distribution of local teaching materials.

Programme structure

The programme is divided into three phases. In phase I the participants will meet for three weeks to learn and practise basic case writing skills. In phase II, they will return to their organisations to prepare a case each. In phase III, the participants will teach their cases, critique the cases of their colleagues and prepare final draft of their cases for publication.

The programme

The participants will engage in the following activities:

Phase   I   -   Introduction to case method; participation in case discussion.

-   Conducting a case method class by participants.

-   Field trips to local industries by teams of participants.

-   Preparation of a writing plan to be implemented in phase II by each participant.

Phase   II -   Participants to work in their local environments writing cases. A draft to be mailed to the programme director at a stipulated date.

Phase III -   Participants to work with the programme director and other participants.

-   Each participant will teach his case, discuss it with the group, prepare a teaching note and finally prepare a final draft that will be presented to the co-operating organisation for release for teaching and publication.

Method of instruction

Instruction in the workshop will involve the use of discussions, lectures, case studies, role playing and other methods as appropriate.

Faculty

The workshop will be directed by ....
Other members of the faculty will be ....

Dates

Phase   I: .... to ....

Phase II: To be announced

Phase III: To be announced

Duration

Phase I of the workshop will require three consecutive weeks of full-time participation and will be residential.

Venue

....

Tuition and boarding

Free, but participants or their organisations are expected to be responsible for their transport expenses. The .... has made a block booking of hotel facilities for participants.

Registration

To register, please fill out the attached application form, giving all information requested and mailing it so that it is received at the .... not later than ....

Confirmation of your acceptance will be mailed or cabled to you soon after.

Further information

For further information contact:
(indicate name, full address, telex and telephone
numbers).

Timetable and instructions for
PHASE I of the workshop
(information for participants)

General instructions

Each week-day will generally consist of three sessions, two in the morning and one in the afternoon.
Each morning session will be of 1 3/4 hours duration.
The length of the afternoon session will vary, depending
upon the session content and purpose.

Morning sessions

Most morning sessions will be given over to case
discussions, each led by a different participant in the
workshop. Typically we will discuss a case for about
one hour, with the purpose of solving the problem raised
by the case. In other words, we will be using "case
method" as teacher and students.

Following the case discussion will come a shorter
period during which, under another group leader, we will
re-examine the discussion experience we have just
finished, with a view to answering such questions as:

1.   What are the teaching purposes of the case and the
     instructor who led the discussion?

2.   How effective was the case in supporting these
     purposes?

3.   How might such a case be used in teaching in this
     country?   In what curricula?   In what specific
     courses?   For what level of students?

4.   Could a locally based case be developed which would
     deal with much the same topic, while being more
     relevant and easier to understand, for local
     students?

In connection with this follow-up examination
(before it, during it or after it) you may want to fill

in a form of the sort called "Case evaluation form", of
which a sample is attached.[1]   Make it a habit to keep a
record of this type in your personal file of cases, and
it will greatly assist you in recalling cases for use
later on.

Afternoon sessions

The focus and content of afternoon sessions will be
more varied, as can be seen from the following timetable.
At times we will be discussing a reading selected from
those issued to you.   At others we will have field
trips, and we will have other exercises as the need
arises.

Small group discussions

From the first day we will form small discussion
groups (similar to "syndicates") which will continue with
the same membership throughout.   Generally, "case preparation" will include some discussion of cases in the
small groups before we meet in general sessions to discuss the cases.

Reading and preparing cases
and readings

When a case or other reading appears in the timetable, it is to be read and prepared before the session
in which it is to be discussed.

(This would be accompanied by a timetable similar
to that shown in Chapter 13.)

---

[1] See Appendix 13.

1. Name of case: _____

2. No. of pages: _____ 3. Industry: _____

4. Country
    referred to: _____ 5. Company
                                     size: _____

6. Major topics or concepts covered: _____

    _____

    _____

7. Is case largely qualitative
    or largely quantitative? _____

8. Short synopsis of case situation: _____

    _____

    _____

    _____

    _____

9. Is this case usable for my purposes? Yes ___ No ___

10. If "yes", in what course or programme? _____

11. If "yes", at what stage of course or programme?
            <u>Early</u>
            <u>Middle</u>
            <u>Late</u>

12. If "no", should I be interested in writing a new case to serve similar purposes?   Yes _____ No _____

13. If "yes" to question 12, in what organisation might I collect such a case? _____

_____

14. Other comments: _____

_____

Cases and notes used in prior workshops

Case or note	Title	Case number[1]	Workshop topic[2]
1	Because Wisdom Can't Be Told (1951)	9-451-005	Chapter 1
2	How to Study a Case (1975)	9-376-661	Chapter 1
3	Managerial Problem-Solving and the Case Method	9-375-822	Chapter 2
4	The Usefulness of the Case Method for Training in Administration (1967)	9-372-105	Chapter 5
5	The Case Method	9-376-896	Chapter 1
6	Business School Objectives and the Case Method of Teaching (1964)	9-375-823	Chapter 6
7	Use of Case Material in the Classroom (1954)	9-354-019 (CR-127)	Chapter 5
8	Pedagogy - Casing Case-method Methods by A.R. Dooley and W. Skinner	Academy of Management Review April 1977, 277-288	Chapter 5
9	The Case Method (A) (1969)	9-373-612	Chapter 1

Case or note	Title	Case number[1]	Workshop topic[2]
10	There's Method in Cases	J.I. Reynolds	Chapter 5
11	Case-Course Development	9-358-003 CR108R2	Chapter 7
12	Writing Business Cases	9-354-007	Chapter 10
13	Some Suggestions for Writing a Business Case	9-355-005	Chapter 10
14	Case Development and the Teaching Note	9-372-733	Chapter 11
15	The Case Method (C) (1969)	9-373-614	Chapter 1
16	Cases Which Meet the Students' Needs (1976)	9-377-844	Chapter 6
17	Preparation of Case Material (1953)	9-451-006	Chapter 10
18	So They're Writing a Case - About You! (1976)	9-376-823	Chapter 10
19	Performance Criteria Used in the Evaluation of Case Course (1962)	9-375-829	Chapter 8
20	Case Method: Its Philosophy and Educational Concept	9-375-614	Chapter 5
21	The Case Method (D) (1969)	9-373-615	Chapter 10
22	Superior Slate Quarry (A) (1957)	HP 236 A(R)	
23	Superior Slate Quarry (B) (1957)	HP 236 B(R)	
24	Superior Slate Quarry (C) (1957)	HP 236 C(R)	

Case or note	Title	Case number[1]	Workshop topic[2]
25	Superior Slate Quarry (D) (1957)	HP 236 D(R)	
26	Vine Dairy Company (1959)	9-505-029 EA-M 376	
27	John Edwards (1947)	9-446-005 ICH DC1H23 EA-A 2	
28	Jason Supply Company (1958)	ICH 3M58R EA-M 347R	
29	Lamson Company (A) (1948)	9-449-003 HP 318R-A	
	(B) (1948)	9-449-004 HP 318R-B	
	(C) (1948)	9-449-005 HP 318R-C	
	(D) (1948)	9-449-006 HP 318R-D	
	(E) (1948)	9-449-007 HP 318R-E	
30	Weston Manufacturing Company (1967)	9-111-047 EA-C 717R Rev. 3/76	
31	The Crown Fastener Company (1955)	9-403-014 EA-A 265	
32	Rennett Machine Company (1956)	ICH DC1C16 EA-C 391R2	
33	Dashman Company (1947)	9-642-001	
34	Gentle Electric Company (1971)	9-672-038	

Case or note	Title	Case number[1]	Workshop topic[2]
35	Allen Distribution Company (1955)	9-201-016	
36	The Case of the Missing Time (1960)	9-408-014	
37	Broadside Boat Builders, Inc. (1971)	9-172-052 Rev. 7/75	
38	Mr. Hart and Bing (1949)	9-403-018 ICH 3H18 HP 324	
39	Voltamp Electrical Corporation	ICH 2G96R EA-G 171R	
40	Shaldon and Sons (1957)	EA-R 56R	
41	Howard Atkins and Joseph Wexler (1956)	9-404-020 HP 469	

---

[1] Unless otherwise indicated, this column indicates that the case is from the Harvard Business School Intercollegiate Case Clearing House, Soldiers Field, Boston, Mass. 02163, USA.

[2] This column refers to the chapters in this manual which will find support in the notes.

Management educators in different languages and in different areas have been organising clearing-houses to encourage the development and distribution of cases and other teaching materials. Many of these case clearing-houses have their own case bibliographies. Each clearing-house is autonomous and develops policies and procedures which best serve its constituents. However, clearing-houses maintain an informal network of communication and co-operation to facilitate the interchange of information among users in different regions and in different languages.

Clearing-houses depend upon individual constituents and their personal bilingual, multicultural professional associates to identify promising cases in the bibliographies and constituencies of other clearing-houses. Each clearing-house depends upon its own pioneers in management education to translate (if necessary) and to endorse and submit those cases which they believe will contribute generally to the constituency of that clearinghouse. Proper authorisation for translation and distribution must be certified. Management educators are encouraged to get in touch with their own clearing-houses for terms on which to contribute new cases and to secure cases and bibliographies.

Addresses of case clearing-houses presently known:[1]

AFRICA (English)

    East African Staff College,
    P.O. Box 3005,
    Nairobi, KENYA

---

[1] Reproduced with kind permission of the ICCH.

Director,
Eastern and Southern African
  Management Institute (ESAMI),
P.O. Box 30301,
Arusha, UNITED REPUBLIC OF TANZANIA

AFRICA (English, French, Arabic)

CAFRAD,
B.P. 310,
Tangier, MOROCCO

Director,
AIMAF et CIGE,
B.P. 322,
Abidjan 07, COTE D'IVOIRE

AMERICAN

Director,
Intercollegiate Case Clearing House (ICCH),
Soldiers Field Post Office,
Boston, Mass. 02163, UNITED STATES

ENGLISH

The Case Clearing House of Great Britain
  and Ireland,
Cranfield Institute of Technology,
Cranfield, Bedford MK43 OAL, UNITED KINGDOM

AUSTRALIAN

Chairman,
Australian Administrative Case Clearing House,
University of Melbourne,
Parkville, Victoria 3052, AUSTRALIA

FINNISH

Director,
Finnish Case Clearing House,
LIFIM (Finnish Institute of Management),
Mikonkatu 19 A,
00100 Helsinki 10, FINLAND

FRENCH

>Director,
>Centrale de Cas,
>108 boulevard Malesherbes,
>75017 Paris, FRANCE

CANADIAN

>Administrative Secretary,
>Centrale de Cas - HEC,
>5780 avenue Decelles,
>Local 440,
>Montreal, Quebec H3S 2C7, CANADA

GERMAN

>Executive Director,
>Zentrale für Fallstudien e.V.,
>c/o Rationalisierungs-kuratorium der
>   deutschen Wirtschaft,
>Gutleutstrasse 163-167,
>6000 Frankfurt/M.11, FEDERAL REPUBLIC OF GERMANY

INDIAN (English)

>Director,
>Administrative Staff College,
>Post Office Box 4,
>Hyderabad-4, INDIA

>Indian Institute of Management,
>Ahmedabad-4, INDIA

ITALIAN

>Scuola di Direzione Aziendale (SDA),
>Universita Bocconi,
>Via Sarfatti, 25,
>20136 Milan, ITALY

NORDIC

>Nordic Case Clearing House,
>c/o The Danish Management Centre,
>Kristianiagade 7,
>2100 Copenhagen, DENMARK

<u>PHILIPPINES</u> (English)

Philippines Case Clearing House,
Asian Institute of Management,
M.C.C. Box 898,
Makati, Rizal D-708, PHILIPPINES

<u>PORTUGUESE</u>

Director,
COPPEAD/UFRJ,
Centro de Tecnologia - Bloco B,
Caixa Postale - 1191 ZC - 00,
20.000 - Rio de Janeiro - RJ, BRAZIL

<u>SPANISH</u>

Biblioteca - CEDA,
Universidad/EAFIT,
Apartado Aereo 3300,
Medellín, COLOMBIA

Instituto Centroamericano de Administración
  de Empresas (INCAE),
Apartado Postal 2485,
Managua, NICARAGUA

Director,
Instituto de Estudios Superiores
  de la Empresa (IESE),
Avenida Pearson, 21,
Barcelona 17 Pedralbes, SPAIN

<u>TURKISH</u>

Executive Director,
Sevk ve Idarecilik Agitim Vakfi,
Cumhuriyet Cad. 279-281 ADli Han,
Haribye,
Istanbul, TURKEY

Andrews, K.R. (ed.): The case method of teaching human
    relations and administration (Cambridge, Mass-
    achusetts, Harvard University Press, 1953).

Bhaya, H.: Methods and techniques of training public
    enterprise managers (Ljubljana International Centre
    for Public Enterprises in Developing Countries,
    1983).

Birchall, D. and Hammond, V.: Tomorrow's office today:
    Managing technological change (London, Business
    Books, 1982).

Blake, R.R. and Mouton, J.S.: Executive achievement:
    Making it at the top (New York, McGraw-Hill, 1986).

Caffarella, R.S.: Program development and evaluation
    resource book for trainers (New York, John Wiley,
    1988).

Christensen, C.R.: Teaching and the case method: Text,
    cases, and readings (Boston, Massachusetts, Harvard
    University, Graduate School of Business Adminis-
    tration, 1987).

Culliton, J.W.: Handbook on case writing (Manila, Asian
    Institute of Management, 1973).

De, N., Flykt, S., Kanawaty, G. and Lindholm, R.:
    Managing and developing new forms of work organisa-
    tion (2nd edition) (Geneva, International Labour
    Office, 1981).

Flamholtz, E.G.: Human resource accounting: Advances
    in concepts, methods and applications (San Francisco,
    Jossey-Bass, second edition, 1985).

Ghosh, S.: Personnel Management: Text and cases (New Delhi, Oxford and IBH Publishing Co., 1980).

Gibson, N. and Whittaker, J.: Results-orientated management development: The case of the Ethiopian management institute (Geneva, International Labour Office, Management Development Branch, 1989).

Gray, J.A.: Cases in management: A select bibliography (Cranfield, United Kingdom, Case Clearing House of Great Britain and Ireland, 1984).

Hayward, G.: Case studies of entrepreneurs in action, with specific reference to the small company (London, Anglian Regional Management Centre), 1981.

ILO: An introductory course in teaching and training methods for management development (Geneva, International Labour Office, 1972). (Revised edition in preparation).

ILO: Building skill and confidence for managing rural development: Cases and exercises (Geneva, International Labour Office, Management Development Branch, 1987).

ILO: Case studies for management development (Geneva, International Labour Office, 1984).

Kirkpatrick, D.L.: How to manage change effectively: Approaches, methods, and case examples (San Francisco, Jossey-Bass, 1985).

Lawlor, A.: Productivity improvement manual (Aldershot, United Kingdom, Gower, 1985).

Leenders, M.R. and Erskine, J.A.: Case research: The case writing process (London, Canada, Research and Publications Division, School of Business Administration, University of Western Ontario, 1973).

McConkey, D.D.: How to manage by results (New York, American Management Associations, fourth edition, 1983).

McLellan, R.: Business policy case studies in Scandinavian companies (London, Anglian Regional Management Centre, 1981).

McNair, M.P. and Hersum, A.C.: The case method at the Harvard Business School (New York, McGraw-Hill, 1954).

Meldrum, B.: Managing employee involvement based on New Zealand case studies (Wellington, New Zealand Employers Federation, 1980).

Nixon, B.: New approaches to management development (Aldershot, United Kingdom, Association of Teachers of Management, Oxford, Gower, 1981).

Ronstadt, R.: Art of case analysis: A guide to the diagnosis of business situations (2nd edition) (Dover, United Kingdom, Lord Publishing, 1980).